THE INVESTING HANDBOOK
FOR ALMOST EVERYONE

THE INVESTING HANDBOOK FOR ALMOST EVERYONE

Gene F. Lee

ISBN-13: 9781981555529
ISBN-10: 1981555528
Library of Congress Control Number: 2017919036
CreateSpace Independent Publishing Platform
North Charleston, South Carolina

For my daughters, Anna and Laura,
as they begin their investing

Table of Contents

Introduction

As you go through life, you will face a series of investment decisions that will determine your future financial well being. Decisions that you need to get right. Are you prepared to make your life's key investment decisions? With the fundamentals you learn in this book, you will be able to make those key decisions knowing you have considered all the relevant factors and possibilities. You can then be confident in your decisions and have investing peace of mind.

This book presents to you the investing knowledge I have learned or figured out for myself over a lifetime of investing and study. In its pages I give you the same advice I have given to my clients during my career as a financial advisor. This book is intended primarily for investors early in your investing life, however experienced investors will benefit as well. Together, we will:

- Discover your investing personality. What traits help or hurt you as you invest?
- Set achievable goals. What is possible, what is illusory?
- Learn the critical value of time and patience in your investing.
- Find reliable information sources and advice.
- Sort out conflicting investment claims and discard media hype.
- Learn how you can research a company and evaluate its stock and bonds.

- Understand what you own in a stock, bond, ETF, mutual fund, or other security.
- Work out your best buying strategies.
- Build your portfolio.
- Minimize your taxes while investing.

This book is instructional and prescriptive to guide you as you invest your money. I recommend that you read from beginning to end and not skip to the topics that grab your attention. The discussions are sequentially organized, and each topic builds on previous discussions.

As you learn more about investing, you may want to take an economics class or an investing class at a local college. College level investment classes will complement what we discuss. However, they won't teach you what you will learn here. Even MBA (Master of Business Administration) finance classes will miss important success factors that you need to learn for yourself.

Part One

Self-assessment
Are you ready to invest

While many of us are eager to make our first investments and many others of us are apprehensive of the unknown, we must all start with the same preparation. The first prerequisite before starting to invest is having an income cash flow above your household needs. What are your family's immediate spending needs? Is your budget under control: Are you living within your paychecks or are you accumulating debt? Whatever your expenses, whether car repairs, private school tuition, or a new roof, get them under control. You must master basic household money management skills before you charge into investing. The money management skills needed for investing are harder and require even more discipline.

The second prerequisite before investing is to eliminate any carry-over debt on your credit cards by paying off the full balance every month. You have little chance of financial success while building up credit card debt as you invest. The typical interest rate charged on credit card debt is much higher than the average rate of return on any viable investment. Eventually, the interest paid on credit card debt will overwhelm your investment returns.

The best situation is to eliminate all debt first, except for a low-interest-rate house mortgage, before you embark on an investment plan. You should understand that accumulating debt is the opposite of investing. When your debts are cleared, then the money once used to pay debt and interest payments can thereafter be used for saving and investing.

Finally, the third prerequisite before investing is to build up your emergency savings, apart from any investments, so that you have an emergency fund. A typical recommendation is six months of living expenses in case you lose your job. Also, you may need to replace health insurance and any other benefits that your former job no longer provides. You need to tailor your savings to your specific situation. If you think that it may take you longer than six months to find a new job in your line of work, then you will need a longer-lasting emergency fund.

Household money management skills are beyond the scope of this book, so we won't discuss it any further here. Once you have taken care of the three prerequisites, you are ready to start an investing regimen.

What kind of investor are you

If you have been investing for a while, you may from your profitable investments and your losses, your successes and failures, have some notion of your strengths and weaknesses as an investor. Whether an experienced investor or just beginning, you must assess your investor personality. This is critically important, because the most easily avoidable investing mistake is a mismatch between your investment plan and your investor personality.

Professional financial advisors will attempt to profile their clients through an interview and a basic questionnaire. They are attempting to determine your *risk tolerance*. However, this technique is limited, because clients simply do not know themselves well enough to answer the questions properly. Inexperienced investors don't know how they will react during an economic crisis.

It is up to you to carefully self-evaluate yourself. Take the time to consider yourself in light of the investor characteristics discussed in detail below. When you are done, you will have a better understanding of your personal investor profile. Your investor personality is the foundation on which to build your investment plan.

Disciplined

Successful investing requires making a straightforward plan and having the discipline to see your plan through without panic. As you will see, disciplined investors have many more strategies available to them. Your success will depend on your ability to carry through with your plan. In later chapters, we will look at the dangers lurking in the marketplace for the unprepared, undisciplined investor. Which have you been up to now? Can you be a disciplined investor? With the right preparation and a bit of courage, yes you can.

You must be disciplined in following an investment plan through to fruition. Or would you sell out the first time a good investment falls in price? What if you have already lost half your money? During the "Great Recession" of 2008-2009, the stocks of many quality companies fell to half their value from their peaks in 2007. Many investors panicked and sold out of the market, some at the very bottom of the market. I know investors who, despite the urging of their financial advisor to stay the course in the market, sold near the market bottom. Peace of mind was more important to them. Later, when the market rose half way back, they felt safe enough to buy back in. By 2013, the market had recovered back to 2007 levels. They were happy that they had gotten out when they did. But I'm not sure that they realized that they lost a quarter of their money, as compared to hanging on to their stocks and then riding the entire upside of the stock market recovery.

Discipline in investing is about courage in the face of adversity. Sometimes referred to as your risk tolerance, courage is your ability to sleep at night while the value of your portfolio drops. If the assumptions and reasons that first convinced you to buy the stock of a quality company remain valid, then unrelated market storms should not dissuade you from your investment plan.

Discipline is more than simply tolerating risk during market adversity. You also must be able to follow through and complete an investment plan during the good times. Once you settle on your investment plan and it succeeds, you must resist selling and spending your investment proceeds prematurely. For example, you must be able to resist tapping into the investments in your retirement fund when your child needs help with a down payment to buy a house. You should save for that special vacation separately from your long-term investment plan and avoid raiding your retirement account.

It's all about planning ahead and carrying out your plan. Yet, no plan can be perfect at the outset; there will be mid-course corrections and emergencies to deal with. Your investment goals shouldn't be so onerous that you give up. We will show you how to set up an achievable plan.

Lack of discipline is the greatest fault in investors. You need to ascertain your ability to stay the course with a solid plan through good times and through economic turmoil until your investment plan achieves your investment goals.

Big-picture versus detail-oriented

Are you detail-oriented with good follow up skills to monitor progress, or are you a big-picture person inattentive to the small stuff? Both styles can be successful but in very different ways. The detail-oriented investor has the potential to actively manage a portfolio of stocks or bonds, monitoring each investment over time. This is especially true investing in an industry where you have some personal expertise that gives you insight and thereby a possible advantage. You may study companies, their products, and business plans to develop an investment story for each investment you make. You will need to watch the companies carefully, attentive to key personnel changes or customer acceptance of new products. However, sometimes such an analytical approach can be overwhelmed by too much data or can lead to overactive trading. We will look at how to sort through the market noise in a later chapter.

On the other hand, a big-picture person may discern the longer term trends in an industry or the economy. You may foresee an economic upturn based on the latest election results or the next market bubble before it bursts. Your insights may take years to play out in how it affects a particular company. For the big-picture person, a passive strategy that requires less direct involvement may be better. Examples of passive strategies would be *buy-and-hold* or *index investing*. We will discuss each of these investment techniques in a later chapter. For this discussion, the theme is that the big-picture person can set a plan in motion and monitor it at the 30,000-foot level. You make course changes in your investment plan at annual or semi-annual reviews, rather than through weekly or daily monitoring of your portfolio.

But don't fool yourself into believing that you are a big-picture person, just because you don't deal with details. To succeed at investing, a genuine big-picture person has to have true insight. You need to be right about the trends, because you will be betting your life savings that you are right.

So what do you do if you are not good at details or you don't trust yourself to spot the important economic trends early? You get help by hiring an investment professional. We will discuss in later chapters where to get investing help and the different ways to hire professional investment help.

Long-term

Are you long-term or short-term oriented? Can you wait years to reap the rewards of your investment plan? Do you want investment results right away in weeks? Would you rather take a quick $20 per share profit or keep a stock for its dividends in your retirement? Your outlook is important because having more time is the greatest advantage an investor can have. Insurance companies, university endowments, and pension funds have a tremendous advantage over the individual investor because they have essentially a continuous investment time horizon. A young investor starts with a huge time advantage that wastes away with age. Younger investors (in their 20's and early 30's) can be, and should be, long-term oriented because they have 35 to 40-plus years before retirement, 35 to 40-plus years to achieve or exceed their goals.

If you are impatient and want to get rich quick while still young, you are short-term oriented. You will need to take extraordinary investment risks to possibly get there, realizing that you may never get rich through your risky investing. You might be better off taking an entrepreneurial route and starting your own business. Put your youthful energy into hard work and grow your business. With your own business, you will have the kind of hands-on control that is unavailable in securities investing.

We will see that long-term investing is all about letting a company make money for you through the conduct of its daily business over the coming years. Investing is not, as many would have you believe, about predicting where a stock's price will be a day, a month, or a year from now.

If you are starting to save and invest later in life, or restarting after suffering a setback, plan with the longest investment time horizon available to you. The more time you give investments to work for you, then the more you reduce the level of risk you need to take in order to achieve a given investment goal. The less time available, the more risk you need to take. It is just easier to achieve a $1,000,000 portfolio, if you have 45 years to do it rather than 10 years. We will discus risk much more later.

Can you be a long-term investor? Life events often dictate our personal time horizon for results; the most predictable are retirement and sending kids to college. Most of the strategies we will discuss favor the long-term investor.

Who do you trust

How trusting are you? No one invests in isolation. You are bombarded daily with market news reports, gossip from friends, advice from brokers, opinions from pundits in the media, and endless advertising with some masquerading as news reports or academic studies. Apart from evaluating the merit of what they say, you have to evaluate yourself for how trusting or skeptical or even gullible you are of others and what they say.

The first source of investment advice for most of us is our parents either by word or example. However, investment ideas that are appropriate for your parents nearing retirement may not be the ideal investment ideas for you just starting out in the work world or with a young family. Your father may be excited by a corporate bond that will pay him a good interest rate for his retirement years, and he may recommend it for you. Well, at least he has your best interests at heart.

Investment advice from friends and family generally is undependable. By the time you hear it, the information will be old and out of date, the opportunity gone if there ever was one. Often they are simply telling stories of their investment adventures, like a vacation story, rather than dispensing thought-out advice for you. They may be bragging about their investments and exaggerating their success. More important, they probably really don't know much about the investment they are recommending, having followed the advice of their financial advisor who may no longer be recommending that idea.

We all seem to know someone who has been a very successful investor for a long time. Someone who may give you an occasional stock tip. Such advice may be worth checking out by doing your own research and deciding if it is a good investment for you. While the investment idea may be well suited to your wealthy friend with an expansive portfolio, that same investment could be too risky and unsuitable for you with a small portfolio. The investment tip may even require a minimum investment amount that is all out of proportion to the size of your portfolio. It would be too large a position for you and thereby too risky.

So "who do you trust"—whom can you trust? Learn to trust yourself. Start simply with the steps presented in later chapters of this book. Start with small dollar amounts because you will make mistakes. Learn all you can, take finance classes, read classic investment books with a skeptical eye. You may decide that you want to add professional help. If so, find an investment advisor and develop a relationship. Determine over time if they are worthy of your trust. Investing is a lifelong learning process, and there are no short-cuts to replace experience. You can, over time, become a capable investor.

Transferable skills

The kind of investor you can be will draw on all of your life experiences. You may already be accomplished in other endeavors. Success and expert skills from other activities can often aid you in investing. If, as examples, you are an engineer, accountant, doctor, or businesswoman, you have certain skills that will help you as an investor. If you are accomplished in music, chess, or poker, you also have some skills useful toward investing. You may be highly skilled in a profession or pursuit similar to one of these examples, if so, then the following respective comments relate to you as well. However, success in any of these fields does not guarantee success in investing. The acquisition of these disparate skills sets for each of these endeavors often come with serious offsetting weaknesses.

Before we look at the transferable skills of these representative subject experts, let's keep grounded by first calling out the two greatest weaknesses of successful people as it relates to investing. The first is believing you are smarter than other investors, than everyone else in the market. You are not. Just take it for granted that you are average as an investor, and it will save you a lot of money. There are lots of very sophisticated investors out there and not necessarily on Wall Street. However, smartness or cleverness is not the most important skill by far—recall the discussion on discipline.

The second great weakness of successful people is overconfidence. As often as not, the overconfidence derives from an "investing system" you have learned or personally developed. The overconfidence comes from some initial self-validating wins and believing that you thereby possess the skills to beat the market. Overconfidence leads to big bets and taking on disproportionately large risks. While your skills have made you a successful engineer or businessman, investing is a wholly different endeavor. Overconfidence while investing is pure folly.

The businessman as investor

Running your own business is a fine foundation for investing. You have a finger on the pulse of your business, your industry, and perhaps the greater economy. You also have the input from your workers, how they are faring in this economy. Business acumen will help you evaluate a target investment. But your most important skill is judicious hiring. You hire experts to add to your own skills. You know how to hire an accounting firm, legal advice, and workers. Your skill in hiring will be meaningful in hiring investment managers. You could learn how to invest on your own, perhaps as a hobby, but likely your time will be better spent running your business. Lack of time and access to information are your biggest handicaps.

The engineer as investor

Engineers are trained to use their scientific knowledge to solve practical problems. As a solution designer it is natural for you to tackle the investment problem. Your ability to study a problem in depth and devise a solution is very applicable to evaluating a company. In fact, I have found most engineers believe they can learn investing techniques and do it by themselves. If you were devote the time to learn, you could become as proficient as many professional investors, with just as wide a distribution of good and bad results.

However, the engineering approach by itself is not sufficient. Engineering is based on experimental science, while investing is based mostly on economics which is far from a science. The engineering solution is grounded in physical world, while the investment solution is always uncertain. Investing is much more a skill of art than engineering. Investing also involves other people; you have to account for the unpredictable behavior of the investing public. But the main practical limitation you face is lack of access to information. The mega mutual fund manager can call a company and speak to the CEO. When you call, you will speak to stockholder relations. Officially, the CEO can't reveal any more information than the stockholder relations spokesperson can, but from whom can you glean more in the tone of their voice or the genuineness of their optimism?

The accountant or doctor as investor

As an accountant, many people ask you for investment advice. That is a natural thing for them do as you handle their taxes and advise on the tax consequences of their finance plans. Your accounting skills are a basic foundation to build on toward evaluating companies. However, the typical accounting task is reporting what happened last quarter or last year and is backward looking at the past health of a company. Investing is about predicting future business results. The investment decision is forward looking and so must evaluate new products and changes in management's strategy. These are additional new skills that must be learned to practice investing.

Similarly, you as a doctor diagnose illnesses using established laboratory test protocols and prescribe established treatment protocols. This in essence also looks back to the tried and true. Your diagnostic skills will transfer to learning to diagnose a company's health. Like the accountant, you will need to learn new skills to diagnose a company's health and predict a company's future business results.

The master musician or chess master as investor

Ultimately, investing is more art than science. Master musicians and chess masters have the ability to find the art in the art of investing. Music is fundamentally mathematical and has a logic all its own. Chess uses paradigm-based applied logic. You are skilled in pattern recognition and in the composition of the elements of your art. Yet to interpret a music score or to find your way through a chess game, you must look at that musical score or chess position and interpret what you see to find or create the themes and ideas buried in the work. The master musician or chess player has a finely honed intuition for their craft, the ability to find the essence of the work. Yours is an acute insight, a cultivated intuitive perception so that you can discern the correct direction to take.

This skill of art I believe transfers to investing intuition. Great investing is much more an art than science—the creation of a successful portfolio results from a composed work of art.

The caution for you in relying on intuition is that you must still do the fundamental economic research on the company, its competitors, and its industry to gain all the understanding you can. But as we will see in later chapters, even the best professionals rely on their intuitive judgment as well as on their analytical abilities.

The poker player as investor

Vital skills you have as a top-notch poker player are the ability to manage your money and to judge when to risk your money. These are also critical skills in investing. However, the application of these skills in investing differs in scope from poker. In investing you never go "all in" where you bet your life savings all on one uncertain outcome. Money management skillfully applied over the years can reduce your loses by appropriately sizing the investment to the risk of the investment. Your poker instincts can guide you to invest more when the investment favors you and invest less when it is riskier. However, judging risk in poker, where you can calculate the odds of winning the hand based on the observable up cards, is much simpler than judging the risk in an investment. Assessing investment risk is extremely difficult. We will discuss investment risk in depth in later chapters.

Perhaps, the most important skill of a top poker player is reading your opponents. Your assessment of the odds in the poker hand is augmented by your read of your opponent and of the strength of his hand. However, it's not at all clear that your ability to read an individual opponent and his hand translates to an ability to read the market. Start slowly by investing small amounts to test your skills.

Your investor profile changes over time

This discussion of transferable skills from various expert skill sets may seem a bit generalized, but it also has the purpose of conveying the wide range of skills that you will need to learn to become a successful investor. Investing as an individual requires a different skill set than that of a professional portfolio manager. This will become clear when we discuss evaluating and choosing investments.

Expect your investor profile to change over time. Certainly, we all grow older and wiser, and our time horizon shortens. You should learn greater investment discipline and patience to become a longer term investor. You will learn to transfer and apply your strengths as a businessman or games woman to investing. You will also need to fill in the gaps in your knowledge and skills. As your needs and goals change, you must be flexible to adapt. In the next chapter you will learn to set appropriate goals.

Setting goals
The vital first step

The first vitally important step in financial planning is setting your goals, that is knowing what you want to accomplish, where you want to be after 10, 20, and 40 years of investing. The ability to set appropriate goals is a learned trait of many successful people. We have all heard stories of people who laid out their life plan and achieved success by following their plan. More often than not, these people had the example of their parents to follow: the children of a corporate executive or doctor who follow their parent's footsteps and themselves become executives or doctors. Setting goals and planning breeds success.

The more specific you make your goals, the easier it is to plan for. "I want to become a mutual fund manager" is more specific than "I plan to graduate from college and get a high paying job." The plan sets you on a clear path. Sometimes it's easier to plan backwards. For example to become a lawyer, you need to go to law school, and before that go to a college whose graduates successfully get into law schools. That in turn means that you need to get good grades, so you know you have to study hard now.

Once you know your goal, you can build your plan. In investing, a typical goal is for retirement income. Your specific goal might be something like "I want to have a monthly income of $9,000 in retirement. And, I want to own my home with the mortgage completely paid off." Now you can set about investing toward those two goals.

Specific, detailed goals are vital, because only then will you know when to switch from investing to accumulate wealth to investing to preserve your wealth. When you first start investing for retirement, you may need to make riskier investments that have the greater potential to grow, for example by emphasizing small-company stocks or even taking a chance on a risky biotech start-up. When you have successfully accumulated the assets to pay off your mortgage and generate $9,000 in monthly income, you will then know to switch to the preservation phase of investing so as not to lose your retirement savings that generates that income. In the preservation phase, you invest in safer bonds and dividend-paying stocks of the most solid companies. If you set a nebulous goal like "I want to retire on a lake in Wisconsin, and help my children buy their first house," you won't know when you have accumulated enough assets to meet your goals and when to switch to the safer preservation phase of investing.

Your goals should motivate you. If you set difficult financial goals, they will motivate you to spend less today and save more in order to have a better retirement. Don't be afraid of setting higher, difficult goals, but they should be achievable. Over the years, as your investments succeed or if you have setbacks, then you adjust your goals realistically.

Husbands and wives should discuss your goals together and agree. It should not be left to only one of you. If, as is often the case, the husband sets the investment goals without consulting his wife and he dies first, the surviving wife may discover that the investment plan does not support her desire to help the children and grandchildren or to travel.

How much to save and how much is too much

There is a trade-off between enjoying life now and saving for retirement or some other goal later. While "Eat, drink, and be merry, for tomorrow we shall die" may be too extreme, there is some truth to "Life is short, start with dessert." When you are young and have the energy and naivete, you should spend enough to engage life fully, if not yet wisely. Since most people don't start saving for retirement until their fifties (which is too late) after their kids have left the nest, this may no longer be an issue for you.

For those young and just starting out and who have the superb discipline to actually save, overly forcing yourself to save may nonetheless be a burden and ultimately counterproductive if you burn yourself out on saving. Start moderately, enjoy youth. For the young adult in their first job, it would be good to pay down student loans and participate fully in the 401(k) retirement plan at work. Above all, do not accumulate debt on your credit cards. Pay off fully all the charges on your credit cards every month. If you can't pay off your credit cards, you are spending too much. As your income grows and you meet your initial goals, set higher goals and revise your investment plan to meet that new goal, such as buying your first house by age thirty.

All the wrong things
to worry about

Missed opportunities

Investing is hard enough without the self-doubt of thinking you have missed out on some great opportunity. Never regret missing the hot stock burning up the headlines or that stock you hear about from friends. There is an old speculator's saying, "Buy the rumor, sell the news." The truth in the saying is, that by the time you read it in the news media or hear it through the internet or from your friends, it is old news. The so-called "smart money" has already bought and is now selling to the late-comers. You are likely already too late. By the way, there is no such thing as the "smart money," there are only people who have access to information faster than you.

If you hear of a hot stock, let it simmer for a while to see if it has staying power. Later, if you are still interested, learn all you can about it, research it thoroughly as you will learn how to do in subsequent chapters.

Beating the market index

If you are making good progress toward achieving your goals, don't worry about beating any stock market index such as, for example, the S&P 500. After all, an index is just a list of stocks, and some investors' portfolios are going to perform above and some are going to perform below a market index, *even if all of you are successfully meeting your goals*. More important than any arbitrary market index is measuring the progress you make toward your own goals.

You may hear some indices referred to as an "average" like the Dow Jones Industrial Average. These indices are not averages in the arithmetic sense. Instead, they are a list of "average" stocks or bonds selected in an attempt to represent the greater market or a single sector, such as the industrial sector. The indices are manipulated with complex mathematical adjustments whenever a stock is dropped from or a stock is added to the index in order to maintain the representational continuity of the index. The indices are useful in helping you follow the trends in the market. Beyond comparing gross trends, the indices bear very little relevance to your portfolio.

Perhaps because we are so used to being graded in school and at work, we feel the need to grade our portfolios. Toward this end, market commentators have turned to indices as a grading standard. This makes fodder for news articles and talking points on TV. Academics and theoreticians have also incorporated index data into their theories. This is more because the data from indices is readily available and goes back many years, than because indices contain any special information. We will discuss the usefulness and limitations of market theories in the chapter on portfolio strategies.

Remember, your goals are what matter and not the stock market indices. You want to take the least risk necessary to meet your goals and not take any unnecessary extra risk just to beat an arbitrary list of stocks in an index. Why take any more risk than necessary to achieve your goals and risk losing on your investments and jeopardizing your retirement? When you are young, you can take more risk to meet your goals in the accumulation phase of investing. After you attain your goals, then you switch to the preservation phase, where you take on much less risk to protect your accumulated assets. When you plan to take lower risk, you can expect to underperform an index, whenever that index portfolio has a higher level of risk.

Setting your goals for others
There will be some goals you wish to stretch for to help your loved ones. If these goals are beyond your reach with a sound financial plan, then you

should set them aside and pay no attention to them, for such goals only serve to distract and confuse you. When you set your goals and plan your investment strategy, you have to take care of yourself and your spouse first. If you are investing for retirement, you may not be able to mix in extra investment goals. For example, it could be next to impossible to invest for the safety of your retirement assets, while at the same time trying to build up an inheritance for your kids. You love your children, and a special needs child may pose a heavy burden with no easy solution. Yet, if you lose the ability to take care of yourself, you won't be able to help a loved one. If your investment plan does exceptionally well in the early years and you see that you will achieve more, then you can reconsider adding to your initial goals.

So relax, set your own goals, make a plan, and execute your plan. Exercise discipline. Most everything else is investment hysteria. We will discuss in a future chapter how to block out the irrelevant noise.

Part Two

Investing basics

Before you learn about stocks, bonds, ETFs, and mutual funds, before you can develop a viable plan for your investments, you will need to understand some basic principles of successful investing. These are canonical ideas that you must accept to succeed. These principles include: 1) the value of time, 2) knowing what do you really own, 3) defining your success, and 4) understanding risk. We will discuss the first three here and devote the next chapter to risk.

Understanding the value of time

Time is arguably the most precious asset we have in life. It is also the most precious asset we have in investing. Our time for investing is limited, and time wastes away with inaction.

The power of compounding earnings

The key to the value of time in investing is the power of *compounding investment earnings*. Let's start with the simplest of investments, where you put $1,000 in a one-year certificate of deposit (CD). Your CD earns, say, 6% *interest* on your *principal*, which is the amount invested. When the CD matures, you add the $60 earned interest to the $1,000 and purchase a new CD for $1,060. You are reinvesting your investment earnings. You will then earn new interest on your principal and the earlier interest together. This earning interest on interest is known as compounding your earnings. When you iterate the process, the compounding builds exponentially. The benefit of compounding applies to all investments where you repeatedly reinvest the earnings so that you receive earnings on earnings.

The reinvestment of the earnings can be in another type of investment besides the original. For example, the interest from the CD could be reinvested in a stock earning a dividend. Then the dividend can be reinvested in additional shares of the stock or in a bond that earns interest. The compounding of earnings continues as long as you reinvest the returns in an investment that continues to earn more.

So, how powerful is compounding earnings on earnings? Very powerful. Table 1 shows three scenarios. The first is where you initially save $1,000 and then add $1,000 in each following year with no interest earned, putting your money in a safe at home. The second is where you initially invest $1,000 in a one-year CD that earns 4% per year. Each year when the CD matures, you add $1,000 as well as reinvest all the interest in a new one-year CD that earns 4%. The third example is where you invest $1,000 in a one-year CD earning 8%, and each year you add $1,000 and reinvest all the interest in a new 8% CD. Table 1 shows how many years it would take you to achieve a goal of $1,000,000.

Table 1 Power of compounding earnings

$1,000 yearly investment	Earning 0% compounded	Earning 4% compounded	Earning 8% compounded
Years to $250,000	250	62	40
Years to $500,000	500	78	49
Years to $750,000	750	88	54
Years to $1,000,000	1,000	95	58

We see in Table 1 the immense power of compounding earnings. The effect is smaller at first but grows exponentially fast in the later years, when the great payoff occurs. With annual contributions of $1,000 earning a 4% interest rate, it takes 78 years to earn the first $500,000. But it only takes 17 years to earn the next $500,000 to reach $1,000,000. The later years of investing are manifestly more critical in building your retirement funds or investing toward any goal. The results with an 8% interest rate are even more remarkable. At 8%, it takes 49 years to reach $500,000 and only another nine years to reach $1,000,000.

You can see that the wealthy really do have an advantage in investing: They are already far out along the compounded earnings time line into exponential growth.

The power of compounding earnings clearly justifies a long-term discipline in investing. If you start early enough, you can reach your goals with investments at lower rates of return like 4% as opposed to 8%. This is important because higher rates of return come with higher risk. Investments that yield 8% are far riskier than investments that yield 4%. Lower risk investments are inherently safer, posing less chance of losing money.

Because the power of compounding earnings starts slowly, it initially takes a long time to build up your principal. This makes it extremely important to start saving immediately and investing as soon as you can get ready to invest as discussed in the earlier chapter. To benefit fully from compounding, you must reinvest all your earnings and not take withdrawals to spend except for dire need.

If you inherit money, you should use it to accelerate your compounded earnings time line. If you add the inherited money, or a substantial portion of it, to your investment portfolio, you can cut many early years from your timetable to meet your goals. The added money will move you closer to the exponential compound earnings power of the later years of your investment time line.

Similarly, if you receive a windfall, such as a bonus at work, use a portion of that money to shorten your investment timetable. You will be able to retire or achieve your other goals so many years earlier. That inheritance or cash windfall should bump you up the retirement investment timetable. It would be a grave mistake to think a windfall realizes all your financial dreams and to start spending it now.

Retirement investment timetable

Retirement plans are designed to maximize the benefit of compounding earnings. Tax-advantaged plans such as the IRA and 401(k) or 403(b) do not allow participants to freely withdraw the money to spend, with few exceptions that are meant for family emergencies. These retirement plans enforce a discipline of long-term investing and compounding earnings on earnings. You should participate and contribute the maximum amount each year. These plans are discussed in more detail in later chapters.

Many people make a serious mistake with their 401(k) plans when they change jobs. They take the money out of their 401(k) and spend it. This cuts off the benefit of compounding earnings. Worse, they will have to repeat the slow-building early years of their retirement plans, adding that amount of time back to their retirement timetable. Taking out all your 401(k) money and spending it is essentially the same as suffering a complete loss in your retirement account, because you have to start over. When you change jobs, keep your retirement plan intact by rolling your 401(k) into an IRA to preserve your retirement timetable—do not cash it out.

In Table 2, let's look at four hypothetical retirement investment timetables. We will assume a constant 4% annual rate of return on investments in the portfolios. We have already seen how an 8% return would yield even more dramatic results, but for these examples 4% will suffice. These timetables can be applied to your IRA, 401(k) or any other retirement plan. (In a 401(k) you would typically make your contributions with your paychecks spread out over time. In order to keep the math simpler, we are assuming here one big annual contribution.)

In the first scenario you start retirement saving on your 25th birthday by making a $12,000 contribution. On each following birthday you contribute another $12,000. Table 2 shows the total savings and compounded earnings available to you if you retire on your 60th, 65th, or 70th birthday. In the second scenario, you begin the same $12,000 annual contributions to your retirement savings plan starting on your 35th birthday. Similarly, the third and forth scenarios begin on your 45th and 55th birthdays. The scenarios then show you the total savings available for retirement on your 60th, 65th, and 70th birthdays.

Table 2   Retirement investment timetable

You begin on your 25th, 35th, 45th, or 55th birthday with a $12,000 contribution. You make annual $12,000 contributions on following birthdays. Assume earnings rate of return at 4% per year. Reinvest earnings for compound earnings. On your 60th, 65th, or 70th birthday you will have:

Savings start age	Retire age 60 with:	Retire age 65 with:	Retire age 70 with:
25	$931,180	$1,197,918	$1,522,447
35	$531,741	$711,940	$931,180
45	$261,894	$383,630	$531,741
55	$79,596	$161,836	$261,894

These scenarios dramatically illustrate the need to start retirement savings early. Study Table 2, along with Table 1. You will conclude that the catchup provision in IRA and 401(k) plans, which allow people 55 years and older to make a slightly larger yearly contribution, is much too little much too late.

Understanding what you really own

When people first begin investing, they are too focused on money. Even experienced investors can be led astray when each month they read their brokerage statements and total up their investment accounts. Keeping track of your investments on a computer spreadsheet, while an important thing to do, only reinforces this misconception of investing as being about money.

How can this be? How can investing be too focused on money? Let me repeat: Investing is not about money. Money is simply the result of investing. Money is there when you are done investing.

How many times have you heard the expression, "We own $30,000 of General Mills?" On the other hand, do you hear anyone saying, "We own $270,000 of house?" No, what you hear is, "We own a $270,000 house." However, in 2009 that house became a $140,000 house. There is no fixed money value for your house. What you really own is *a house*. Similarly, as an investor, you may believe you own $30,000 of General Mills (GIS), but then the next day when its price changes you don't own $30,000 of General Mills. What you actually own are *600 shares* of General Mills stock. On any given day, at any given moment, the price of a share of General Mills stock may be, say, $50 or not. For that transient moment when the price is $50, your GIS stock is worth $30,000, but you still actually own 600 shares of General Mills stock, and you will own 600 shares of GIS the next day. You don't own $30,000. To experienced traders, that transient $50 price is known as the *spot price* of GIS, which is the price you get at the moment of purchase or sale—on the spot.

Mutual funds, like stocks, also are sold as shares. So you own shares of a mutual fund. The price of a share can change daily. An oddity of mutual funds is that you can buy and sell fractional shares, so that you could own 200.345 shares of a mutual fund. This is possible because you buy and sell mutual fund shares only with the mutual fund company itself.

ETFs, which trade like stocks on exchanges, are traded in whole shares. However, some brokerages provide a dividend reinvestment service that allows you to reinvest dividends and hold fractional shares of an ETF or a stock in your brokerage account. This is a bookkeeping service where the brokerage allocates fractional shares to you from stock and ETF whole shares owned by the brokerage in its own account.

With bonds you own individual bonds. However, bonds have a *par* value that can complicate things. When a bond is newly issued, it has a face value known as par value. A typical par value is $1,000. So when someone says they bought "a $50,000 bond," they are actually referring to buying a quantity of 50 bonds at a par value of $1,000 each. What they really own are 50 bonds. The actual cost to purchase the bonds was based on the transient spot price at the time of purchase, that being 50 times the spot price, which may not equal $50,000. So while they say they own "a $50,000 bond," they actually own a quantity of 50 individual bonds. And tomorrow they will still own 50 bonds, regardless of changes in the spot price and the value of the bonds.

So, the important concept to understand is that you own shares of stock, shares of a mutual fund, shares of an ETF, and individual bonds—these are your assets. Never a dollar amount of stocks, mutual shares, ETFs, or bonds. Understanding this concept will help you withstand market swings in prices and the monetary value of your portfolio. When you look at your statement and see that you still own 600 shares of GIS stock, 200.345 shares of your mutual fund, and 50 bonds, you can be reassured that not all that much has changed despite the daily and monthly changes in market prices.

When the Dot Comm bust occurred in 1990-2000, investors took huge losses, just as they did again when the financial credit crisis hit in 2007 and caused the worst recession since the Great Depression. These losses were in the hypothetical values of their portfolio. However, they still owned the same number of shares of stock and number of bonds as they did before the bubbles burst, unless they sold in panic. Investors with a long-term perspective held on to their shares of stock and their bonds. Eventually, the market recovered as did the hypothetical value of their portfolios.

Understanding what you really own can prevent the beginner mistake of focusing too much on money.

Understanding the value of what you own

The value of your investments is straight forwardly calculated. For each asset, the value is the quantity you own times the current price. Add up the value of each asset and that is the value of your portfolio, which is all your assets together. Yet most people are confused about the value of their investments.

Imaginary losses and unrealized gains or losses

Most people find brokerage statements obtuse and confusing, so as a result many people ignore the details in their statements. Statements can be overly complicated, and even after all these years I still find my statements difficult to read. Rather than ignoring your statement or just looking at the dollar total for your portfolio, what you want to look for is the list of what you own, the list of your assets. Your assets' dollar values may fluctuate, but it is your assets that make up your portfolio. What you own won't have changed until you buy or sell shares of stocks, shares of mutual funds, or individual bonds.

When you tally up your portfolio in the evening, you take the closing price of each asset at the end of the day's trading session and use that price, along with the quantity, in calculating a value for your portfolio. That calculated value is the hypothetical value of your portfolio at the end of the day. Similarly, your broker dealer calculates a hypothetical value for your portfolio and prints it on your monthly statement. The hypothetical value is usually stated with the designation "as of" or "as of the end of" as in the example "$287,000 as of March 31st." By the time you actually get your statement, the value of your portfolio will have changed, because the price of the assets you hold will have changed. The printed prices are no longer the spot prices. The printed "as of month end" portfolio value is no longer timely.

Even with an automated online portfolio statement using the latest prices, the values are hypothetical. For by the time you actually go to sell a stock, the spot price will have moved. The speed of online trading notwithstanding, your sell order will be executed behind earlier orders in the sequence received. The spot price could change in the interim.

Now suppose years ago you bought your 600 shares GIS stock at $40 per share for $24,000. Today your brokerage statement reports a price of $50 per share and a hypothetical total value of $30,000. You have a hypothetical increase in value of $6,000. This $6,000 is called a *paper gain* or, more formally, an *unrealized gain*, meaning it's not real until you actually can sell your shares of stock for $50 per share. An unrealized gain represents a potential profit, while an unrealized loss represents a potential loss.

Your brokerage account is very different from your bank account. In your bank account, there you own *dollars* at cash value—a hundred *dollars* is valued at $100. In your brokerage account you focus on shares of stock rather than the hypothetical money value. In looking at your brokerage statement, the number that is constant and accurate is the number of shares. The number of shares is constant until you sell some shares or buy more. You constantly own 600 shares of GIS, you don't own $30,000.

Your brokerage account statement shows a hypothetical value for each asset. Each hypothetical value imputes an unrealized gain or an unrealized loss for each asset depending on whether the price today is higher or lower than your purchase price.

Why is this distinction so important? It is important because we as human beings fool ourselves into believing we own more value than we actually have. This happens because the spot price is constantly changing, so as a consequence the value of the asset is constantly changing. We fool ourselves because we fixate on and remember the highest hypothetical value we have seen on our statements. Suppose your 600 shares of GIS hit a high price of $70 with a high value of $42,000 as of the statement from three months ago and have dropped to $50 with a value of $30,000 as of the last statement. Then we worry that we have lost money from that high value of $42,000, despite the fact that it was nothing more than a fleeting, transient value, a snapshot in time. Because these hypothetical values appeared on our official statements, we actually think we have lost $12,000, despite the imputed $6,000 unrealized gain. However, neither the imaginary loss of $12,000 nor the unrealized gain of $6,000 is real. The $12,000 imaginary loss will never be real, but the $6,000 unrealized gain has the potential to become real if you actually sell GIS for $50.

When you choose to sell your 600 shares of GIS stock, you first check the price and if $50 is satisfactory you place a sell order, either though your broker or online. The order is transmitted, your stock is sold almost immediately (during market hours) for some spot price usually close to $50, and you will collect approximately $30,000. So what was an unrealized gain is now realized upon the sale for a real profit of approximately $6,000. Now you own approximately $30,000 in cash.

Chasing imaginary value

The perception of this imaginary loss causes many bad investment decisions. In particular, people try to avoid this imaginary loss and will wait for their stock to recover back to the peak level before selling, trying to recover to an imaginary value, you might say. We all face this temptation. However, the stock may take months to recapture the peak or may never reach that level again. Once you decide to sell a stock or bond because it no longer meets your criteria to hold it, you have essentially decided that the stock or bond is no longer desirable or even safe to own. Any delay in selling it exposes you to a higher risk of losing money going forward from your decision point. When you make a sell decision, then sell and take your unrealized gain or unrealized loss and forget about imaginary loss.

For many people an imaginary loss comes from an imaginary value that they believe they once owned. But the imaginary loss was never real and likewise the imaginary value was never owned and is not worth keeping track of. Any effort to recapture imaginary value is foolish and a distraction from what is realizable and important. People who chase imaginary value will always feel like they have lost money, even when they have an unrealized gain for the taking if they were to sell. This is a basic novice mistake—not accepting the true value of what you own, which is the number of shares multiplied by the latest price. By avoiding this mistake, you won't be too euphoric in a wild up market or too panicked in a recession.

Understanding success
in investing

You define your own success

So if it is not all about money, what defines successful investing? By now it should be clear to you that you get to define your own success in investing. You decide what goals are important to you. You establish the milestones to measure your progress. If you are ready by the age of 25 and start investing, you have met an early milestone of success. As you invest toward your goals, as you pass milestones, as you achieve your established goals, you are succeeding in investing. When you have met your goals, you have succeeded. And if you have had to adjust your goals along the way to reflect the 2008-2009 economic recession, that was only realistic and practical. Success is meeting your goals.

At times we let our competitive natures get the better of us. We want our investment returns to be as good as or better than that of our neighbors or coworkers. We want to beat the S&P 500 market index, or beat the so-called "comparable index" shown on our brokerage statements. However, investing should not be a competition, it is not a race. Just as you work to be able to live and enjoy life, you invest for your goals—to send kids to college, to retire by a target date, to live and enjoy retirement.

Investing as a hobby

Some folks find that they enjoy the activities of investing: studying stocks or bonds, reading books and articles on investment strategy, tracking the value of their assets, and picking "winners." Investing becomes their hobby.

All well and good. However, set apart your investments that are dedicated to your life goals in their own inviolate investment account. Set up a separate dedicated account for your hobby of investing. I have heard these hobby accounts rightly called "my play account." You may wonder, "What's the difference, since I want to pick the best stocks for both accounts?" The reason is that hobbyists tend to be active traders. As we will discuss further in the chapter on investment strategies, active trading is not a recipe for success.

Your results as a hobbyist, that is as an active trader, will be up and down; this in the profession is call *volatility*. Higher volatility is associated with higher risk. Treat your hobby of investing as you would if you played in a regular poker game—for you are doing just that. Fund your hobby with entertainment money. In your hobby of investing, don't play with any more money than you can casually lose and feel no pain. If you score a big win with your hobby, take that lucky bonus out of your hobby account and add it to your investment account. Never take money from your investment account to put in your hobby account. Never treat your investment account like your hobby account. It's not worth the risk and the pain.

It is now time for a thorough look at risk.

Risk

One of the most important concepts in investing is that of *risk*. Risk signals danger and causes fear, and fear inevitably causes a response. Before we begin to invest, we must come to terms with how we face investment risk. Risk for primitive man came from anything that can hurt you. The primitive response to that fear was to flee. In modern society, we fear things that can go wrong: the risk of disasters, chaos, war, and economic depression. The civic response is laws, government, and militaries. In investing, the risk is from the chance that you will lose your money. In facing investing risk and fear, our first instinct is to revert back to our most primitive flight response, sell and flee.

You cannot be a successful investor from a posture of fear. Time and again, fearful investors make the irrational decision to flee. Your brave response is discipline. Educate yourself and get professional help if you need it. Review the previous discussion on discipline.

You must understand risk in all its aspects in order to understand investing. Risk is unavoidable in investing. Risk results from the uncertainty of future prices, unpredictable outcomes, and unforeseeable events that affect our investments. Risk also arises from the unpredictability and the irrationality of human behavior, both our own and that of the everyone else who participates in the market. We can not control the risk factors that a business faces. You can only prepare for uncertain events by implementing risk mitigating strategies within your portfolio. You will learn how to prepare for risk in the discussion on investment strategies.

Personal investment risk

What is risk in investing? The pertinent definition of risk for you as an individual investor is: the chance that you might lose money on one specific investment or on your portfolio as a whole. So for our discussion, we mean your personal investment risk, the chance that you might lose money when you sell an investment that you currently own or are buying. This practical definition is how you and I as individuals view investment risk.

In later chapters, we will find that economists in their investment theories use another definition for risk that doesn't align so well with the perspective of individual investors. They equate risk with *volatility*. This academic view of risk as volatility aligns more with the attributes of financial institutions with their professional investors, and not so well with us as individuals.

What causes risk

Any business or investment has inherent risk. The company you invest in may fare poorly or even go bankrupt or out of business. This is the *business risk* associated with your investment. Business risks can be identified. In fact, business risks are always discussed at length in a company's *annual report*. Any public company listed on the stock exchanges is required to issue an annual report, as well as quarterly reports. A key step in investigating a company is reading its annual report, paying particular attention to the discussion of business risks. The annual report will discuss every risk that management can identify. This includes *development risk* from the uncertain success of new products such as an experimental drug in research and development (R&D) that may fail to cure its target illness, *competitive risk* from competitors' products that customers may buy instead of your company's products, *legal risk* where the company may be sued over defective products, and every other risk a company faces.

Risk factors vary greatly from one investment to another; some investments are considered very safe, while others are known to be riskier. As an example of a safer investment, short-term United States government bonds that pay back the principal plus earned interest within 52 weeks are known as Treasury bills or T-bills and are considered among the safest of investments. The full taxing power and borrowing power of the U.S. Government back up its promise to make T-bill payments as they are due. Similarly, banks offer certificates of deposit which, subject to certain dollar limits, carry Federal Deposit Insurance Corporation (FDIC) insurance. The FDIC is backed by the full faith and credit of the United States government, so CDs backed by FDIC insurance are also among the safest of investments.

On the other hand, a speculative investment in the very cheap defaulted bonds of a bankrupt company, where you hope to reap enough pennies on the dollar in the bankruptcy court settlement to make a profit, is obviously extremely risk and only suitable for hedge fund speculators and the very wealthy. Also, an investment in the stock or bonds of a troubled company attempting a turnaround to fix its problems is among the riskiest of investments. And, an investment in a new, unproven start-up company with no products yet on the market is very risky.

In between these two ends of the risk spectrum, candidate investments abound for you to investigate and judge the risk taken versus the potential reward. These include the stock of large multinational corporations that span the globe, the stock of railroads, miners, media companies, and so forth, as well as the stock of new companies with unproven products. You can also consider mutual funds, municipal bonds offered by cities, and ETFs. As we discuss each type of investment asset in later chapters, we will highlight the risks specific to that investment type as well as its potential for reward.

Learning how to evaluate an investment's risks is a key skill of investing. This can only be learned by doing. As you make your first investments, you will inevitably suffer losses from misjudging an investment's risk. Don't let this discourage you. Too many people prematurely give up on investing after they suffer their first losses. Just keep your early investments small while you learn to judge investment risk.

Risk and reward

Risk is such an integral part of investing that the decision to buy an investment is often framed as a balancing of risk versus reward. You seek to buy an investment at a price where your likelihood of a gain exceeds the risk of a loss. If the risk of an investment is higher, you need a lower price to offset the likelihood of loss. If the risk of an investment is lower, you could pay a higher price and still likely make a gain. This is the risk-reward trade-off in investing.

The risk-reward trade-off is one of the two key dynamics that drive the pricing of investments. The other is supply and demand. Supply-and-demand action results from the competition among buyers and sellers. When the supply, which is the quantity for sale, of a bond is large, it is more difficult to sell them all, so the seller lowers the price to attract more buyers in order to sell more bonds. When the supply is low, the seller can demand a higher price for the few bonds that are available. On the other side of the trade, when the demand for a bond is high, buyers are looking to buy more of them, so a buyer in order to be sure to get the bonds must be willing to offer a higher price than the next buyer who may not get any at all. When demand is low, people are looking to buy fewer bonds, so buyers can offer a lower price to willing sellers.

Risk-reward and supply-and-demand are interrelated. The level of demand will depend on each buyer's separate assessment of the risk-reward trade-off. Demand is the aggregate of the buy decisions of individuals. Conversely, the level of supply is based on the risk-reward assessment of the individual sellers. Dynamic markets result from buyers and sellers coming to differing conclusions about the risk-reward trade-off of investments.

You will encounter risk-reward discussions often as you learn more about investing and as you read reports about individual companies. Risk-reward is a key concept in portfolio theory, which we will discuss under investment strategies.

Your risk tolerance

We alluded to your personal risk tolerance in the discussion of discipline in investing. In your self-evaluation, you may have found it hard, particularly if you are new to investing, to say what your reaction would be to bad news about a company you have invested in or to a precipitous drop in its stock price. Your own reaction to such bad news is referred to as your *risk tolerance*. If you can hang in there and wait and see before deciding what to do, you have higher risk tolerance. If you want to sell quickly and not allow it to get worse, then you have low risk tolerance. Neither reaction is good or bad, better or worse than the other, it simply is how you behave. You have to make your investment plan while cognizant of your own personal risk tolerance.

If your own likely reaction is unknown to you, that in itself is an element of risk: your own unpredictable behavior risk. In that case, it is better to assume you have a lower risk tolerance as you start investing, because most people overestimate their ability to withstand uncertainty and a drastic drop in the hypothetical value of their portfolios. This can be a serious misself-perception. They will hold out during a steep price drop—down 5%, 10%, 25%, 40%, and more—only to give up suddenly and sell in a panic. Better to have sold earlier at the first signs of discomfort.

If you have low risk tolerance, then you want to focus more on safer, conservative to moderate investments that have less chance of a sudden, big price drop. These include various types of bonds and the stocks of big, established companies, sometimes called blue-chip companies. You can shift the balance of your portfolio toward these conservative investment assets and away from riskier small companies, foreign stocks, or speculative investments. However, you may still want to keep a small portion of riskier investments in your portfolio as they have a higher potential for reward.

You will also have to keep your goals realistic and aligned with what your moderate-conservative portfolio can achieve.

On the other hand, if you have high risk tolerance, you can consider moderate to more aggressive investments that carry higher risk with their greater potential to gain in value. So, you would look at smaller companies, international stocks, and even a few new companies, investments with high reward potential. However, you will also want to keep a solid base of safer investments to stabilize your portfolio from wild, extreme swings. Having high risk tolerance does not mean it's okay to be foolhardy just because you can tough it out. There still is no reason to take any more risk than necessary to meet your goals.

Your risk tolerance is a very individual, personal trait. It can also vary widely from one investment to another, particularly where you have expertise in a given industry. For example, if you are a battery expert, you may be able to evaluate better the impact of a new innovative energy storage technology from a new company on the battery company you currently own. You may realize the new technology is too unstable to be safely used in cars, and it will not displace the old battery technology. Your risk-reward assessment will result in greater confidence in your current battery company. So your risk tolerance for a drop in the price of its stock will be very high, as you perceive any drop to be temporary and the price will recover. Your risk tolerance in the old battery company will be higher than your risk tolerance in other less familiar industries.

As you gain experience investing in both good and bad economic times, during both bull (rising) and bear (falling) markets, keep track of how nervous or uncomfortable you may have felt with the various assets in the your investment portfolio. Try to gain a greater understanding of your own reactions and risk tolerance. Also keep in mind, your risk tolerance will change as you gain experience, meet your goals, and near retirement. Typically, it will drop as the preservation and safety of your portfolio become paramount.

Part Three

Types of investment assets

To achieve success as an investor, you will need to develop an investment plan that meets your investing goals. Your investment plan must fit your investor personality and risk tolerance. You will determine the appropriate investment assets, selected for safety, that fit into your plan. In this section we examine the characteristics of the primary investment *securities*, such as stocks, bonds, mutual funds, and ETFs. In later chapters we will discuss investment strategies and how to select and buy stocks or bonds. We will also look later at how to organize your investment assets in a portfolio of complementary securities to implement your strategy. In a later section on tax planning we will discuss the IRA, 401(k), pension plans, and tax considerations in investment planning.

The great variety of investment products offered to you can be very confusing. This is true even for experience investors and for professionals who tend to have narrow, specialized expertise. In order to sort them out in your mind, it may help to think of your investment asset choices like a buffet table: Bonds and stocks are the meat and vegetables, mutual funds and ETFs are like casseroles, options are utensils, and alternative investments are like wine. Investment programs such as the IRA, 401(k), and pension plan as well as your brokerage account are the pots and bowls that hold investment assets. Annuities are like prepackaged frozen dinners.

Certificate of deposit

The *certificate of deposit* (CD) is issued by banks and sold by banks and their distributors such as brokerages. CDs are a popular investment with retirees and also with young investors as their first investment just starting out. CDs earn steady interest and are relatively uncomplicated and easy to buy. Most important, CDs are guaranteed by the Federal Deposit Insurance Corporation (FDIC), an agency of the U.S. Government, when issued by a member bank and below the FDIC dollar limit.

In purchasing a CD, you are in fact lending your money to the issuing bank. The bank promises to pay you interest, periodically or at maturity, and to repay the loan at maturity. As an investment, CDs are a debt instrument of the bank, like short-term bonds which they resemble. With a CD you own a promise of interest and repayment of principal by the bank in the form of a promissory note.

FDIC insurance

The FDIC insurance is the main reason for the popularity of CDs. As a result of bank failures during the Great Depression, the federal government in 1933 established the FDIC as an independent agency to stabilize the U.S. banking system. Member banks of the FDIC must follow strict regulations and can issue FDIC insured CDs. The current limit on FDIC insurance is $250,000 for the combined dollar amount of all the deposit accounts of one person at one bank. Amounts in CDs and other deposit accounts totaling above the limit are not insured. The amount above the limit is backed just by the bank itself. You should always verify that any CD you buy is in fact FDIC insured and that the combined total of your deposit accounts at one bank is below the limit.

However, it is possible to set up multiple account ownership in such a way that you can get combined coverage in excess of the $250,000 limit. Let's look at two examples assuming only CDs for the sake of discussion. First, and simplest, if you as an individual have more than $250,000 that you wish to place in CDs, you can buy CDs at several different banks, with the total amount in CDs at each bank below the FDIC limit. The total of your FDIC protection is then only limited by the number of independent banks (not branches of the same bank). Second, if you are married, you and your spouse can each own CDs in your individual names at one bank and your individual CDs will be protected up to the limit separately. This would insure $500,000 combined. You can also open a joint account in both your names, which is separate from your individual accounts, to protect an additional $250,000 each in the joint account. So in this example, the total you and your spouse can invest and protect at one bank by opening properly titled CDs would be $1,000,000. Your two single accounts and the joint account are in separate "ownership categories" as defined by the FDIC. The limit is applied independently in each separate ownership category. FDIC rules can be intricate, so work with the bank to verify that all your funds in CDs in these multiple ownership accounts qualify fully for the FDIC guarantee.

CD pros and cons

FDIC insured CDs have the premier benefit of safety. They are as safe as treasury bills, since both are fully backed by the U.S. Government. CDs have an advantage over most other debt instruments in that they are issued to you at a fixed interest rate so that you know exactly what you are getting. Also, the interest available on CDs can go up slightly when you invest a larger amount. When you purchase a "Jumbo" CD with a $100,000 minimum investment, it will be issued to you at a higher interest rate than smaller CDs from the same bank.

While the safety of FDIC insured, interest-paying CDs is very comforting, CDs do have one key risk. That risk is that your money is locked up in the CD and unavailable until the maturity date. This is called *liquidity risk*, where your money can not be withdrawn and available whenever you want it. The longer the CD is issued for, the greater the liquidity risk. So, for example, if you purchase a five-year CD with an interest rate of 4.7%, and two years later interest rates jump up to 6.2%, your CD will still be locked up at 4.7%, and you will not be able to switch to a higher interest rate for another three years. The inability to access your money to take advantage of opportunities or pay sudden expenses is liquidity risk.

Because of their familiarity with CDs and because of the FDIC guarantee, investors often overrely on CDs. It is not unusual for retirees to have almost all their savings in CDs out of fear of losing money. While this may be fine if you already have sufficient funds to last the rest of your life expectancy plus ten years, many retirees instead worry that they will run out of money. At times CD interest rates may not keep up with inflation, so they are not effective investments to build up your retirement savings. Generally, the role of CDs in your portfolio is as a place to park money for a brief time while you wait to use the money or while you build your cash position toward a larger investment. For longer periods, you can consider a mix of bonds at better interest rates.

Bond

Bonds are issued by private companies, government bodies, and private institutions, for example a university, to raise money for their operations. Most bonds are distributed through investment banks and brokers for sale to investors.

When a company needs to raise money, it can issue either bonds or stock. Bonds and stock are very different from each other. Bonds represent a debt obligation of the company that must be repaid to the bondholder. Stock represents proportional ownership of the company by the stockholder.

When you purchase a bond, you are lending your money to the bond issuer. You own a promise from the issuer in the form of a promissory note that it will pay periodic interest and repay the principal to you on the maturity date. As such, a bond has a limited life and represents a debt of the issuer that will come due. Upon maturity, the issuer repays the principal, and the bond is retired.

People buy bonds for their constancy and relative safety. Bonds pay you a fixed interest rate, typically quarterly, for the life of the bond, so in retirement you can rely on bonds to provide a steady stream of income. A bond's value may swing up and down over the years, but at maturity you can depend on a high quality, investment grade bond to pay you back the face (par) value of the bond, so you know the exact amount you will receive.

Bond interest rates

When looking at bond interest rates, you must distinguish between the fixed interest rate that a bond pays, the bond's variable *yield*, and the *prevailing interest rate*. A bond is issued with a fixed interest rate known as its *coupon rate* or *coupon*. A bond's coupon is set by the issuer when it is issued. For example, the coupon might be set at 5.00%. The issuer will pay to the bondholder an interest payment equal to the coupon rate times the bond's face value, which is called *par*. A $1,000 par value bond with a 5.00% coupon will pay interest of $50 per year, typically distributed in quarterly payments. The coupon rate and par value will not change over the life of the bond, so the interest you are paid is also fixed.

Your initial yield from a bond is based on the cost of the bond, which may be below (at a discount to) or above (at a premium to) the par value. The current value of any bond is set by supply-and-demand and will fluctuate as sellers and buyers trade that bond. As the bond's value changes, the bond's calculated yield will also change. Your bond's current yield is the coupon amount divided by the bond's current value. For example, a $50 coupon from a bond with a current value of $950 will yield 5.26%. Market forces will keep the bond's yield close to the prevailing interest rate.

The prevailing interest rate is determined from the most recent bond trades in the market place. The prevailing interest rates are typically quoted for archetype bonds such as, for example, the 10-year treasury or the 10-year, AA, municipal bond or the 5-year, A, corporate bond. The prevailing interest rate will fluctuate and at any moment may be higher or lower than the coupon rate of the bond you own. Suppose you own a 25-year, AA corporate bond with a 5% coupon. The current value of your bond will be set by the trades of other bonds similar to your bond. The value of your bond will be set by the market such that the yield on your bond will be very close to the prevailing interest rate.

Bond ratings

Bond ratings are based on the creditworthiness of the bond issuer and, hence, serve as a guide to the safety of the bonds. They help you select from the multitude of bond choices. Bond ratings are important to the issuing company, because the rating is used in determining the coupon rate the bond pays to investors, and this affects the ongoing cost of the bond to the company. The highest bond rating is **AAA** which is reserved for the few most creditworthy bonds. The company itself may come to be labeled "triple A," however the bond rating applies only to the specific bond being rated. A bond's rating only serves as a guide to the safety of the bond; the rating does not serve as a guide to whether the bond is expensive or cheap.

Bonds suitable for individual investors like you and me have one of the top four ratings which, in order from the top, are **AAA, AA, A**, and **BBB** (or **Baa**). Bonds with one of these four ratings are considered *investment grade* bonds. Investment grade bonds are safer because they are issued by creditworthy companies who are less likely to have trouble and default on their bond payments. (Bond ratings may be fine tuned with a "**+**" or a "**-**" modifier, such as **A-** or **BBB+**. The modifier may be numeric with "**1**" or "**2**" or "**3**," such as **Baa2**.)

Bonds with ratings below investment grade, such as **BB+, Ca**, or **D** are *speculative* grade bonds, also known as *junk bonds*. The poorer quality and higher risk of junk bonds mean the issuing company will have to pay a higher coupon rate to attract buyers, which in itself places a greater financial burden on the company. While companies who issue junk bonds may encounter no trouble and pay their bonds on time, they are nonetheless at much greater risk to default on a bond payment. Leave speculative junk bonds to the professional bond traders.

Bond ratings are issued by various rating agencies such as *Moody's* and *Standard and Poor's* (S&P). The bond rating reflects the rating agency's best judgment of the bond issuer's creditworthiness as well as the bond's rank in the order of claims. The same company can issue different bonds with different ratings based on varying maturities and on whether the bond is secured or unsecured. The bond rating may change over time with the changing fortunes of the issuing company. So you need to check your long-term bonds regularly to see that they are maintaining their ratings. Also, the rating agencies may disagree and give the same bond differing ratings, for example an **A-** from Standard and Poor's versus a **Baa1** from Moody's.

Bond issuers pay the rating agency to rate a new bond when it is issued. Because the rating service is paid by the bond issuer, this obviously sets up a potential conflict of interest for the rating agency, as the issuer wants a high bond rating. So, the rating agencies work diligently to maintain their objectivity and reputations.

Because of the cost of procuring a rating, some issuers will forgo a rating and issue an unrated bond. This is sometimes the case with municipal bonds issued by local governments. The issuer is relying on its reputation in the financial market to drive sales of its bonds. An unrated bond, however, may end up paying a higher coupon rate than it otherwise might if it were highly rated.

Corporate bond

The corporate bonds issued by a company are considered safer than the stock of that company. This is because the payment of interest and principal to bondholders has a prior claim to the cash of the company above dividend payments to stockholders. In the event a company fares poorly and has a cash shortage, the interest due bondholders will be paid first, and, if there is cash left over, then the dividend due to stockholders will be paid. If the company should go bankrupt, bondholders will have prior claim over stockholders to the proceeds from the sale of the company's assets. All the bondholders will be paid in full first, before the stockholders receive any payment at all.

A company may issue many different bonds over the years, and each series of bonds may differ from the others. Bonds can vary in time from issue date to maturity date, amount of coupon interest paid, and priority of claim on the cash and assets of the company. When you purchase a bond, it will have an established place versus other bonds in the priority order of their claims on the company's cash and assets.

Corporate companies can issue secured or unsecured bonds. Secured bonds are backed by specific assets owned by the company and pledged toward the payment of that bond first. The pledged property can be capital equipment, real estate, or the stock of a subsidiary of the company. Unsecured bonds are backed by the ability of the company to make good on its promise to pay and by the assets of the company that have not been pledged. Unsecured bonds can be subordinated to other unsecured bonds, thereby establishing a priority hierarchy in the order of claims.

In evaluating a corporate bond, you will want to understand the ratio of the company's cash flow compared to the cash required to pay interest and principal coming due. You will also want to look at the overall level of debt owed by the company compared to stockholder equity. These debt ratios are widely available in the business media and are calculated from the annual report and other official statements filed by the company. You can compare the company's debt ratios to those of other companies in its industry. The ratios will vary greatly from industry to industry. Utilities companies and telecommunications companies are heavy issuers of corporate debt, because they have large dependable cash flows from providing an essential service. Young computer technology companies typically have little debt.

U.S. government bond

When it needs to raise money, the United States government will issue bonds to investors. Historically, bonds were issued in times of war. Now days with regular government budget deficits, bonds are issued continuously to support the operations of government. The national debt is the accumulation of the outstanding federal bond debt.

The U.S. government issues basically three kinds of treasury bonds: *treasury bills*—with a short maturity up to 1 year, *treasury notes*—2 to 10 years, and *treasury bonds*—more than 10 years; collectively referred to as U.S. treasuries. (U.S. Savings Bonds are too limited to be used as investment vehicles.) In purchasing treasury securities investors are loaning money to the U.S. government; the bonds are direct obligations of the federal government to pay interest and repay principal at maturity. The U.S. treasuries are backed by the taxing power of the U.S. government, as well as the further borrowing power of the federal government during times of budget deficits. And ultimately, because the U.S. controls its own currency, the treasuries are also backed by the power of the U.S. government to print money. (Note that this is not true for bonds of Euro-currency countries which do not control their own currencies and cannot individually print money.)

By virtue of the strength of the U.S. economy, treasury bonds are considered the safest investment, deemed with no credit risk by consensus in the investment community. As such, U.S. treasuries provide a solid bond investment choice to anchor and stabilize your portfolio. U.S. treasuries have the added benefit that the interest income is not subject to state and local taxes, although it is taxed by the federal government. When we discuss investment strategies later, you can consider a mix of treasuries and high grade corporate bonds for part of your portfolio.

U.S. treasuries historically had always been rated the highest **AAA**, but in 2011 one rating agency dropped its rating one step to **AA+**. In practice, the only current threat to the creditworthiness of treasury securities is the political risk of Congress not acting in time to appropriate money to pay the bond principal and interest. This has never happened, but the confrontational political brinksmanship in Washington, D.C., of the past decades has undermined confidence in U.S. treasuries. Longer term, the continuing federal budget deficits will erode U.S. economic strength and could hurt the creditworthiness of the U.S. government.

In addition to U.S. treasury securities, the U.S. government has created various agencies and government-sponsored enterprises that have issued bonds, such as the Government National Mortgage Association (Ginnie Mae), Federal National Mortgage Association (Fannie Mae), Export-Import Bank, Student Loan Marketing Association (Sallie Mae), and the Farm Credit System, among others. The securities from these agencies and enterprises have varying levels of U.S. government backing—no guarantee for some bonds—and have varying tax benefits.

Agency issued mortgage-backed bonds are very complex. They differ from other types of bonds in their maturities and in how they repay the principal. Because these agency mortgage-backed securities are so varied and complex, you should seek expert help before investing in them. I do not recommend them for beginning investors without professional help.

Municipal bond

Municipal governments such as the states, cities, school districts, water districts, hospital districts, flood control districts, mosquito abatement districts, and a host of other local agencies can issue municipal bonds to raise funds. Municipal bonds represent a debt obligation that has to be repaid by the municipality. There are literally thousands of different municipal bonds that could appear in the bond marketplace for you to choose from. Some are well known such as Los Angeles School District bonds, others are obscure such as a bond from a local school district in Nebraska.

Municipal bonds come in two types depending on the source of repayment funds. *General obligation* (GO) bonds are backed by taxes levied by the municipality. A bond tax may be approved by the voters in a local election and become a component of the overall property tax bill of residents of a local district or city. Additional municipal tax sources are business, sales, and excise taxes. The other type of municipal bond is the *revenue* bond. A revenue bond may be issued to fund, for example, building a bridge, an airport, or a public hospital. The revenue bond is backed by bridge tolls, passenger and airline fees, or the hospital's business income, respectively.

Like corporate bonds, municipal bonds can have a bond rating from the various rating agencies such as *Moody's* and *Standard and Poor's*. Again, the investment grade ratings are **AAA**, **AA**, **A**, and **BBB** (or **Baa**). Though a corporate bond might have the same rating as a municipal bond, you should not equate an **AA** corporate bond with an **AA** municipal bond. The two classes of bonds are too different to simply compare ratings together. For example, municipal bonds may be insured, as well as backed by taxes.

Municipalities can purchase bond insurance from private bond insurers to augment the safety of their bonds and thereby lower the coupon rate the bond will need to attract investors. The addition of insurance can bump up a municipal bond from its innate underlying rating of, for example, **BBB** to a higher rating of, say, **AA** as an insured bond. In the event that a city is unable to pay the interest or the principal of its insured bond, the bond insurance company will step in and make the interest or principal payments on schedule in place of the city to the bondholders. Thus, the creditworthiness of the insurance company is added to the creditworthiness of the city. The bond issuer is motivated to purchase insurance, because the higher bond rating means the bond will need to pay less interest, enough so that the savings more than cover the cost of the insurance.

Depending on the state where you pay tax, municipal bonds may receive favorable tax treatment. Typically, a state will exempt interest income from municipal bonds issued in that state, but it will tax interest income from municipal bonds issued in another state. You should check the municipal bond tax rules in your state. When a municipal bond is free of both federal and state taxes, it is referred to as *double tax-free*. Note that some municipal bonds do not qualify as tax-free and can be taxed. You should always verify with your broker the taxable status of any bond you are considering. Also, some municipal bonds can trigger the alternative minimum tax (AMT) on your federal tax return. Another question to ask your broker is whether a municipal bond is susceptible to the AMT.

The double tax-free (and AMT-free) municipal bond is very popular because it saves on taxes. Your tax savings is greater if you are in a higher tax bracket. Accordingly, the price of the double tax-free bond is bid up by higher-income people willing to pay more to get the tax savings. As a result, the yields on municipal bonds are usually lower than the yields of taxable bonds of similar maturity. Whether you will save enough on your income taxes to make up for the lower amount of interest you will receive from municipal bonds depends on your tax bracket and on your individual tax situation. You will need to consult with your tax advisor to determine if investing in municipal bonds makes sense for you.

Par value and bond pricing

Bonds have a face value called *par*. The par value is the amount of principal that the issuer of the bond will repay to the bond owner upon maturity to settle the debt that the bond represents. Earned interest is paid in addition to the principal. Par value is used to calculate the actual cost to you of a bond investment. A typical par value is $1,000. When you go to buy a bond, the price will be quoted as a percentage of par as follows: If a $1,000 par value bond is quoted at a price of 102.30, then the cost to buy the bond is $1,023. The cost is 102.30% of par, which is 1.0230 times $1,000. Similarly, if the price is 98.90, then the bond will cost $9,890. The cost is 98.90% of par, which is 0.9890 times $1,000.

So, let's say you want to invest $15,000 in bonds, which would be a quantity of 15 bonds at par of $1,000 each. You identify a bond that you like with a price of 101.30. Your cost will be 1.013 times $15,000 par which is $15,195. You will have to kick in an additional $195. Or you can buy just 14 bonds for $14,182 to stay within budget.

(Though people conventionally say a $15,000 bond, they technically mean 15 individual $1,000 par value bonds. Likewise, a $100,000 bond is really 100 bonds of $1,000 each.)

When you give the order to buy that $15,000 bond be sure to make clear whether you mean an outlay of $15,000 cash for the bonds or, instead, you mean a par value of $15,000 which could result in a cash outlay of more or less than $15,000 depending on the price of the bond. Always ask the total cost to you of the nominal $15,000 bond.

A bond purchased for a cost above par value is called a *premium bond*, and the *premium* is the amount above par value, $195 in the example above. Similarly, a bond purchased for a cost below par value is known as a *discount bond*, and the amount below par value is the *discount*. A premium bond will pay a coupon rate above the prevailing interest rate. The premium is to pay for that higher coupon rate. A discount bond will pay a coupon rate below the prevailing interest rate, and the discount is to offset the lower interest paid.

The purchase cost determines the bond's yield. The yield is equal to the coupon rate times the par value divided by the purchase cost. Or figured another way, the yield equals the amount of interest paid to you in a year divided by the purchase cost to you.

How bond prices are determined

You may be wondering why the cost of a bond is not simply the par value and the price is not just 100.00. The price you pay for a bond is determined by two market forces: *risk versus reward* and *supply-and-demand*. We introduced these concepts in the chapter on risk, now let's see how they work in the case of bonds.

When you want to compare the risk of different bonds, you can easily determine the risk associated with a given bond by looking at its bond rating. The rating agency will have performed the complex task of evaluating the creditworthiness of the issuer. The higher the bond rating the safer the bond, and investors such as pension funds, institutional endowments, insurance companies, as well as individuals will be willing to pay a higher price for that safer bond than for a lower rated bond. With more risk, a lower rated bond will have to offer a lower price or more interest before you would want to buy it. Hence, the reward for accepting more risk and less safety is a higher yield.

Another way to look at it is to compare the coupon interest rates. An **A** rated bond will have to pay more interest than an **AA** bond to attract a buyer, since given the choice and all else being equal, you will pick the safer **AA** bond. To make the higher risk **A** bond more attractive to you and me, the issuer will have to pay a higher interest rate to compensate for the higher risk, thereby adjusting the risk-reward ratio to be comparable to that of the **AA** bond. Adjusting the risk-reward ratio to attract buyers manipulates the demand side of supply and demand.

Bond prices and interest rates move in opposite directions

From our discussion above, you should take special notice of how bond prices and prevailing interest rates move in opposite directions. This opposite movement seems at first counter intuitive, until you completely understand bond price movements. You might reread the previous bond pricing discussion specifically studying this opposite price and interest movement.

This inverse relationship applies to bonds you own. When the prevailing interest rate goes up on comparable bonds for sale in the market, the price you can get for your bond will go down. This happens because the coupon on your bond is fixed. When the prevailing interest rate goes up, say, 30%, your fixed coupon can't go up 30% to match it, so its relative value suffers. Conversely, when the prevailing interest rate goes down, the price you can get for your bond will go up, because your coupon stays fixed at its relatively higher level. This inverse relationship between bond prices and prevailing interest rates is well-known.

The drop in bond prices and values in response to a rise in prevailing interest rates is known as *interest rate risk*. You will need to be aware of interest rate risk when you consider bond purchases.

Bond spreads

We mentioned earlier that U.S. treasuries are considered to have no credit risk. As such, U.S. treasuries serve as the standard to which all other bond interest rates are pegged. The interest rates of U.S. treasuries are called the *risk-free rate of return*. The interest rate of other types of bonds can be thought of as being composed of two components: the risk-free rate of U.S. treasuries of similar maturity plus an added incremental rate to compensate for the bond's added risk. This increment is called the *spread*, and a bond's spread is calculated by subtracting the risk-free rate from the bond's interest rate. As an example, Table 3 shows how the spreads might look for various ten-year bonds on any given day.

Table 3 Example of bond spreads for ten-year bonds

Ten-year bond	Interest rate %	Spread %
U.S. treasury	2.32	---
Corporate AAA	2.72	.40
Corporate AA	2.95	.63
Corporate A	3.21	.89
Municipal AAA	2.10	-.22
Municipal AA	2.22	-.10
Municipal A	2.48	.16

In looking at the spreads in Table 3, we can readily see that the 10-year, AA, corporate bond is paying 0.63% more than the 10-year treasury. We also see that the 10-year municipal AA bond yields 0.10% less than 10-year treasuries. This is because the municipal bonds are double tax-free and with this advantage can offer lower yields, despite not being risk-free.

Bond spreads are a simplified way to compare bond interest rates. In discussing interest rates in terms of spreads, we subtract the treasury rate component and highlight the movement of the incremental interest component for each archetype bond. You most likely are already familiar with the use of spreads from sports. Sportscasters may declare a college basketball team to be a 4-point favorite over their opponent. This is the point spread of the anticipated final score, be it 75-79 or 103-107. The financial media will often talk in the simplified terms of spreads.

Bond spreads are often quoted using a bit of investment jargon: 100 *basis points* (BPS) make up 1%. So 0.63% is the same as 63 basis points, and 10 basis points is 0.10%. It's no different in concept than in baseball where a 300 batting average means getting a hit in 30% of your at bats, and batting 1,000 is getting 100% hits. In the fractional percentage range of spreads, the use of basis points is merely a handy phrasing.

Bond maturity and calls

Bonds are a loan that must be repaid when due. That repayment is due on the *maturity date*, set when the bond is issued. At its simplest, a bond is much like a CD: The bond is issued, bought by an investor, pays interest, and repays the loan upon maturity.

Some bonds have an added feature to protect the issuer if prevailing interest rate were to fall before the maturity date. These bonds have *call* dates on which the issuer can choose to recall the bond for early repayment. There can be one or multiple call dates. If prevailing interest rates fall, the issuer is motivated to issue new bonds while recalling the older bonds. The new bonds will pay a lower coupon rate, saving money for the issuer. The older, higher coupon bonds are repaid using the proceeds from the new bonds, which for the issuer replace the older bonds. Since bonds will only be called when it saves the issuer money, the bond owner will lose a high yielding bond and be faced with no way to replace it. Any bonds currently for sale will yield near the prevailing interest rate which will be lower. This risk of losing the higher coupon rate of the older bond is known as *call risk*. Part of the process of evaluating bonds is assessing the call risk due to the potential for prevailing interest rates to drop during the life of the bond leading to a call.

Given a choice, all else being equal, a buyer would choose a bond without call provisions. In order to entice investors to buy callable bonds, the issuer may offer a slightly higher repayment upon a call, in essence sharing some of the savings with the bondholder. For example, the call price may be 101.00 for the first ten call dates and 100.00 for the later call dates closer to the maturity date. Other issuers may offer a slightly higher coupon for a callable bond compared to a noncallable bond. The repayment premium above par or the higher coupon is meant to offset somewhat the call risk.

If you buy a callable bond with a higher coupon than comparable noncallable bonds and your bond is never called, you reap the bonus of that higher coupon. Such bonds are referred to as *kicker bonds* (or *cushion bonds*) for the extra "kick" that they provide to your return. Some savvy bond investors look for potential kicker bonds. Potential kicker bonds can be identified by comparing the *yield to maturity* (the yield if the bond is never called) to the *yield to call* (yield at a call date) or *yield to worst* (the lowest yield from any call date); the yield to maturity will be higher. Your bond broker can help with this assessment.

At a level of maximum complexity, there are some bonds with flexible maturity dates and some bonds with variable interest rates set at auction. There are even perpetual bonds that only pay interest and never mature. Some examples are bonds from the U.S. government agencies mentioned previously, as well as institutional bonds from investment companies. These complex bonds are constructed with the help of lawyers to protect the issuer and are, therefore, risky for you. They are extremely difficult to understand and evaluate even for investment professionals. They are best avoided by individuals like you and me and left to the professional bond traders at financial institutions.

Bond liquidity

The ability to sell an asset immediately without suffering a price drop is called *liquidity*. Both individuals and corporations place cash in the safety of bonds, buying and holding bonds to earn interest until the money is needed, when they want immediate access. This is possible because the bond market is huge, both in the trillions of dollars of trading volume and in the literally thousands of separate, distinct bond issues outstanding. U.S. treasuries are easily bought and sold, and there is active trading in bonds from large, creditworthy corporations, utilities, and municipalities. Because of their safety, U.S. treasuries are among the most liquid of bonds. You want to be able sell bonds quickly when you need access to the cash, but during a market crisis buyers may suddenly become scarce, suspending their activity. In that situation you may have to offer a large discount at a very low price to find a buyer to raise needed cash. This risk of losing money from not being able to sell in a timely manner or even sell at all is the essence of *liquidity risk*.

Even in a normal market, it can be difficult to sell a little known, long-held bond. A bond that was once well known and popular, over the years, can fade into obscurity. You may not even find a buyer, in which case you may be forced to hold that bond to maturity to recoup your principal at repayment. The bond should continue to pay interest, but your principal will be unavailable for other uses. You should periodically review your bond holdings with your bond broker or advisor and perhaps sell bonds that are not aging well.

Liquidity risk can be avoided by carefully planning your cash flow from bond maturities. One way to do this is by timing the maturity of your bonds to match your anticipated cash needs for major expenses like buying a house or college tuition. We will discuss several timing strategies in the chapter on how to buying bonds.

Stock

When people talk about investing, usually the topic is stocks. The dream is to find the new wonder stock that will soar and make you rich. For now, we will put off the discussion of getting rich with stocks to the chapter on stock investment strategy and here look at what you buy and own with stocks.

A corporation issues stock to raise money for use in its business. A new business will start small owned by the founders. Later, the company may incorporate and sell *shares* of stock to investors to raise working capital to grow its business. When you invest in stock, you buy part ownership of the company and hold *common stock*. Stockholders are also known as shareholders. Investing in stock is sometimes called investing in *equity*, which is the remaining value of the company after subtracting its debt. All the stockholders together own the company in proportion to their share holdings, the founders having received an initial allocation of stock. The stockholders elect the company's board of directors who are responsible for running the company for the benefit of the stockholders.

As an owner, you can profit from your stock investment in two ways. The first is when the company pays a dividend from its earnings to its shareholders. The second is when the company uses some of the earnings to grow the business which adds to the equity value. The increasing equity value will eventually push the stock price up.

Corporate stock actions

The total number of shares of stock will vary over time due to various corporate actions. For example, additional stock can be issued and sold, the stock can be split, or the company can buy back stock.

In a stock split shareholders receive additional shares of stock from the company. For example, in a two-for-one split each shareholder will receive one additional share for each share currently owned, resulting in his owning two shares versus one share before. The stock price will adjust down by one half, so that the total value of the shares owned before and after the split remains the same. Any dividend is similarly adjusted down, so that the total dividend paid remains unchanged. However, a stock split is sometimes accompanied by a dividend increase, so that the total dividend after the split will be higher than before. Since every shareholder will have twice the number of shares, a stock split does not change the percentage of the company each shareholder owns. A growing company with a rising share price will split its stock primarily to keep its share price affordable for the average investor. Periodic stock splits also convey the notion of company growth.

When a company has excess cash, the company can buy some of its own stock in a stock buyback. Buying back stock reduces the number of shares outstanding and, over time, increases the value of the remaining shares outstanding. Stock that is bought back is stored in the company treasury for future resale to the pubic or for issuing to reward key employees.

Dividend

A *dividend* is a distribution of the company's profit to its shareholders. Companies usually declare and pay dividends quarterly, though some companies pay semiannual or annual dividends. Also, a company could pay a one-time special dividend, if they have cash from an extraordinary event like selling a subsidiary. Dividends are paid per share of stock, so your number of shares times the dividend rate gives your total dividend. Not all companies pay a dividend, particularly younger companies using all their resources to grow.

Dividends come out of a company's cash flow and profit. Cash flow is the more immediately critical of the two. One of the key steps in evaluating a company and its stock is looking at whether the cash flow can sustain the dividend payments. With sufficient cash flow, a company can continue to pay dividends while weathering a troubled economy even if it is temporarily unprofitable. A company must have cash flow to pay the bills, while profit is an accounting calculation subject to interpretation, deferrals, and perhaps manipulation. Unlike bond interest which must always be paid, dividends can be reduced or suspended in times of extreme corporate hardship. This potential loss of the dividend is one reason a company's stock is riskier than its bonds. A cut in the dividend is a certain sign that the company is dealing with severe problems.

Income stock

As an investor, you want to look for a strong steady dividend from a company to provide you income. A reliable dividend stream provides a measure of safety in the investment. Ideally, the dividend amount grows regularly. An increasing dividend is a sign that the company is doing well and that management feels the increase is sustainable. Be careful to look for a rising dividend cash amount as opposed to a rising dividend rate. A rising or excessive dividend rate could be the result of a falling stock price, which can be another sign of potential trouble at the company.

The growth over time of the dividend is one advantage of income stock over bonds in generating retirement income. The increasing dividend can keep up with inflation, while a fixed interest payment will fall behind inflation. However, a company must make interest payments before dividend payments, so its bonds are deemed safer.

What about companies that don't pay a dividend? Not paying dividends is a cautionary sign. In the worst case it means a company is not profitable and in trouble. Or it could mean a company is only getting by and not profitable enough to pay a dividend. Both these types of companies should be avoided, as you will get neither dividends nor share price growth. The only time not paying a dividend is acceptable is when the company is growing its equity value and its stock price is steadily appreciating.

Growth stock

Companies that rapidly grow their equity value reward their stockholders through high stock price appreciation. In a young and growing company, management may choose to plow profits back into the company to further growth and stock value. In management's judgment the cash is better used to develop new products, hire and train new employees, and build a sales force. This growth should then be reflected in an increasing stock price. Many young exciting companies start out not paying dividends only later to pay a respectable dividend. Examples in high tech include Intel, Microsoft, Apple, and Oracle.

Investing in a non-dividend-paying growth company is inherently riskier than investing in a dividend-paying company. A dividend-paying company has established a reliable cash flow, and you receive a current return on your investment. With a non dividend-paying stock, you expect to build up unrealized gains above your purchase cost, and these gains will only be realized when you sell the stock. This is riskier because you are putting off your return. If the company's growth stalls, you may see a large drop in the stock price and a corresponding drop in the unrealized gain, possibly even falling to an unrealized loss. See the discussion earlier on imaginary loss and unrealized gain or loss.

You as an investor must decide for yourself based on your risk tolerance how to balance growth stocks in with the dividend-paying stocks in your overall stock portfolio. You decide if a growth company's potential stock appreciation is worth more than receiving a dividend from an investment in another company. Based on your own risk profile, perhaps an investment in a company that pays a moderate dividend and also has moderate growth prospects would be a good compromise. You will find that companies run the spectrum in their blending of paying dividends and funding growth. Typically, a well-managed company will have several cash-generating product lines as well as new product lines that need cash infusions to build growth.

Once you decide that you can tolerate the greater risk inherent in growth companies, growth stocks provide a potentially higher return for that risk. When you are young, allocating a significant portion of your investment portfolio to growth companies potentially can boost you along the compound earnings timetable.

Stock value and price

The price of a stock is much more difficult to evaluate than the price of a bond. This manifests in the greater price swings that you see in stock prices compared to bond prices. Fundamentally, the two market dynamics of balancing risk versus reward and of supply and demand that we described for bond pricing also apply to stock pricing. Because of the greater risk of stocks with the potential of losing substantial sums of money, the pricing of stock requires a thorough evaluation of risk versus reward.

In the pricing of a stock, dividends contribute one component to the stock price, analogous to the bond coupon in determining a bond's price. However, since stock conveys ownership of a business, the stock price has additional components of value that must be taken into account. The price of the stock includes the value of the fixed assets of the company such as factories, equipment, and real estate. The company also owns valuable intangible assets such as brands, patents, and intellectual property. The company has value in its reputation and in the quality of its workforce and management. The accounting statements that you find in the annual report attempt to place dollar values on these various corporate assets and attributes. Also, the company has value in its ability to grow its revenue and earnings and to grow its dividend to shareholders.

Every potential investor in a stock makes their own evaluation of these components of value. Different investors and stock analysts will value these components differently. Some investors will highly value the dividend, while others will assign more value to the company's revenue growth. Then, the sellers will offer a range of *ask* prices and the buyers will offer a range of *bid* prices on the stock exchanges. The *spot price* that you can get at the moment of trade is set at the intersection of these two ranges where the bid price matches the ask price. In practice, you as seller or buyer will see the bid price or the ask price, respectively, either online or from your broker, and you will decide whether to conduct the trade. When there is no agreement on bid and ask, no trade can occur. The *bid-ask spread* is the difference between the bid price and the ask price. The next trade will occur when a higher bid arrives or a lower ask arrives such that there is an agreement on price. That trade sets the new spot price.

However, in evaluating stock value remember that you need to keep focused on the products, the quality of employees, and the business prospects of the company. As we said at the outset, investors can become too focused on money and stock price movements rather than on the fundamental business potential of the company. Investing in stock means owning a piece of a living business. We will discuss in detail evaluating a company and its stock in the section on how to pick and buy stocks.

Target price

Target prices are widely quoted in brokerage stock reports and in analyst or pundit interviews. As you read company reports from brokerages, you will see stock analysts discuss many of the components of value and declare a *target price* for the company's stock, usually what they think the stock price will be 12 months hence. Unfortunately for us looking for guidance, different analysts may disagree widely on their assessment of the prospects for a company, on the components of value, and, hence, on their target price for its stock. They may even disagree on whether a stock price will go up or down. And analysts will likely revise their target prices well before 12 months pass. This should be a strong clue to you not to place too much credence in target prices. You should treat a target price as merely a summary of the analyst's opinion on the company and not as any valid predictor of future prices. You should not depend on target prices in choosing stocks to invest in.

Price earning ratio—P/E

There is no substitute for thoroughly studying and understanding a company in deciding whether to invest in the company and at what stock price. That is the difficult job of trained professional stock analysts. One useful analytical tool is the *price earnings ratio* or the *P/E*. The P/E is a basic comparison of a stock's price to the company's earnings. Because the P/E is relatively easy to explain, it is useful for encapsulating and communicating stock analysis. It is popularly quoted by both analysts and media commentators. Because the P/E is so widely discussed, and at the risk of oversimplifying stock evaluation, we will explain how to use the P/E, with the understanding that it is only one tool in the stock analyst's kit.

You can easily look up a stock's P/E in the stock tables published on the internet, along with the current stock price and the day's trading range of high and low prices. If you want to calculate the P/E yourself as an exercise to understand it, you would first determine E, which is the earnings per share of stock during the past twelve months, using the company's quarterly reports. Then you take P, which is the current stock price, and divide it by E. The result is the P/E ratio of the stock.

When the E used in the calculation is the earnings per share from the past 12 months, the P/E is described as the *12-month trailing P/E*. One of the tasks of analysts is to predict a target stock price. One forecasting method an analyst will use is to calculate a variant P/E using his own estimate of the company's earnings per share for the next 12 months with the current stock price. This forward looking P/E is referred to as the *forward P/E* or the *forward 12-month P/E*. If the forecasted earnings go up, then the forward P/E will be lower, and vice versa. If you further assume the P/E will remain fairly constant over the next 12 months even as the estimated E goes up, then future P will have to go up. The future P thus calculated from the estimated future 12-month E would be the new target price. Thus, the forward P/E and the target price are closely associated.

However, the P/E cannot always be assumed to remain constant. The P/E can change due to events at the company. For example, if the company introduces a hot new product, that product success can justify a higher stock price in the minds of buyers as they anticipate more revenue and earnings. That higher price would raise the P/E before the anticipated earnings are realized. In this case, a high P/E could indicate a fast growing company.

Generally, it is useful to compare the P/E of a company to that of other companies in the same industry. Also, you can track a company's P/E over time to see if it has risen or fallen. A higher or lower P/E by itself is never a definitive buy or sell signal; it can indicate either an opportunity or a warning. You have to study the company and find the reason for the change in the P/E to determine if it is a buying opportunity or a warning to sell or avoid the stock. As much as anyone might wish otherwise, the P/E is not a decision-making panacea.

When a company's P/E is lower than the P/E of similar companies, that may be an indication the company is undervalued with a low stock price. The stock is cheap relative to the other companies. You have to determine why the stock is cheap. It may be that the company's main product has consistently lost sales to the competition, so the company is falling behind and its stock price has fallen. Or, the company may have suffered an industrial accident, from which the company will eventually recover, as would the stock price. The stock price may be depressed but should go back to its previous level. This may be a chance to buy the stock at a temporary low price.

When a company's P/E is higher than that of the competition, it means the company stock is relatively expensive. Again, you have to determine why. If a company is growing rapidly, people will buy its stock in anticipation of greater earnings and this results in the stock price going up and the P/E going up. Or, maybe people are too eager to jump on the bandwagon and have bid the price up way too high, far ahead of any future earnings. Then the stock price may be set up for a fall, when the earnings eventually disappoint stockholders. You need to figure all this out to decide whether to buy or sell or avoid.

Analysts and commentators are fond of discussing the 12-month forward P/E and their underlying assumptions. As they bandy P/Es, you can become confused. Read and learn from their analyses and commentaries, examine their key assumptions, and watch how they use P/E or future P/E, thoughtfully or fast and loose.

Preferred stock and convertible bond

As the financing needs of corporations have gotten more complex over time, their investment bankers and lawyers have created categories of security assets that combine features from both common stocks and ordinary bonds. These hybrid securities are the *preferred stock* and the *convertible bond.*

Preferred stock offers a fixed dividend that has priority over the common stock dividend. Preferred dividends are paid after bond interest and before common dividends. The common dividend will be cut before a preferred dividend is cut. A major added attraction of some preferred stocks is that their dividend is *cumulative.* That means if the company misses paying a cumulative preferred dividend, it must make up all the missed cumulative preferred dividends before any other dividend can be paid. This added protection is attractive to income seeking stock buyers.

A convertible bond pays interest and has the added feature that the bondholder can choose to exchange it for stock at a preset conversion ratio, such as, say, 20 shares of stock for 1 bond. For a $1000 par value bond that 20:1 conversion translates to $50 per share of stock. If the stock price subsequently rises above the $50 conversion value, the bondholder can convert and benefit from the stock appreciation. Convertible bonds often pay a lower interest rate than the company's regular bonds, using the ability to exchange for stock as an enticement for the bond buyer.

Generally, a company will issue preferred stock or convertible bonds when it needs to sweeten the deal to attract buyers. This may be the case when the company's regular stock price is very low, and the company doesn't want to sell additional common shares at that low price, diluting the value of the stock. It could instead issue preferred stock with a higher priority dividend at a higher price. When a company doesn't have sufficient cash flow to pay a high coupon interest on a new bond issue, it can offer a convertible bond at a lower coupon rate. If the price of the company's stock later goes up and the bond is converted, then it would essentially be as if the company had sold stock earlier at the higher conversion price.

These hybrid features make determining the risk and the price of a preferred or a convertible just that much more complicated. These hybrid investments are best left to professional institutional traders. The investment professionals at an insurance company or a mutual fund can fit these hybrid products into the risk distribution of their vast portfolios using computerized asset allocation models. We, as individual investors, can instead buy a simpler mix of common stock and ordinary bonds, each being easier to price than a complex hybrid security.

Bankruptcy

Always be alert for news of sudden trouble at a company in which you own stock or bonds. Companies in apparently good health can fail with shocking speed, for example if the main factory of a food processing company is irrecoverably contaminated. If a company you own is suddenly in deep trouble and threatened with bankruptcy, don't panic, but act immediately to gather all the facts and decide if you should sell, and if so, sell quickly. In bankruptcy, the stockholders will lose all of their investment, the stock becoming worthless. Though bondholders are paid first when company assets are sold, bondholders may get pennies on the dollar.

Bond *covenants* often trigger a pending crisis. A bond covenant is a condition in the bond *indenture*, which is the bond contract between the company and the bondholders, imposed on the issuing company to protect bondholders. A covenant might say, for example, that the bond must be repaid before the issuing company can merge with another company. Or, the covenant may specify that the bond must be paid immediately in full if the company fails to meet certain financial tests. For a troubled company, failing these financial tests and being unable to repay the bond debt to meet the covenant can force it into bankruptcy.

As an individual investor, never buy the stock of a company in trouble as its stock price tumbles. Even if you are certain the company will recover and you think you can make a big profit, in almost every case you don't have enough information and likely will lose money. Always wait for the company to actually return to health before thinking of investing in it. You may miss making a rare killing, but it's not worth the greater risk of losing your money. Always leave bankruptcy investing to the professional hedge fund traders. Unfortunately, many investors need to learn this lesson the hard way.

As an owner of stock or bonds of a corporation publicly traded on the exchanges, you can only lose as much money as you have invested in the purchase cost of the company's stock or bonds. You are shielded from any liabilities of that bankrupt corporation, unlike someone who own a business individually or in a partnership.

Stock exchange

Most companies are listed on one or more stock exchanges. Two major stock exchanges in the U.S. are the New York Stock Exchange (NYSE) and the NASDAQ (National Association of Security Dealers Automated Quotations). The bidding of prices for the trading of stocks takes place on the exchanges, which enforce trading rules designed to maintain an orderly market. The stocks of companies listed on the major exchanges are usually very liquid. The stock exchanges provide ready buyers and sellers for listed stocks. When your buy or sell order is placed, it will generally execute within seconds (during market hours).

The stock of some very small companies may not be listed on an exchange and instead trade over-the-counter (OTC), which is not a regulated exchange. Small OTC stocks may not be so liquid, without ready buyers or sellers, and trades may take longer to execute.

When a company's stock is first listed on an exchange, it is cause for celebration. The stock is given a *ticker symbol*, such as GIS for General Mills or INTC for Intel. Conversely, a company can be delisted from an exchange. Sometimes the company has been acquired by another company, and the acquired company's stock is retired. Other times, a company can fall on hard times and no longer qualify to maintain its listing per the rules of the exchange. It is delisted and then trades on another exchange where it may still be listed, or it may trade over-the-counter.

The stock exchanges are themselves private companies. They are regulated by the U.S. Securities and Exchange Commission (SEC), which is the government body overseeing the securities industry, the stock exchanges, and other securities organizations.

The stock exchange is an example of a *secondary market*, where investors go to trade their securities. Stocks, bonds, options, and other securities are traded on secondary markets. The *primary market* is where issuers go to raise funds from investors. For example, the *initial public offering* (IPO) of stock from a start-up company occurs on the primary market, thereafter the stock is traded on the secondary market.

Each major country has its own stock exchange where the stock of companies from that country is traded. Large multinational companies can be listed simultaneously on different foreign exchanges. The stock of some large foreign companies can be purchased on U.S. exchanges in the form of *American depository receipts* (ADR). The ADR is issued by a U.S. bank which holds shares of the foreign company's stock. Each ADR represents some fixed number of the shares of the foreign stock on deposit at the bank.

Mutual fund

We discuss here the most common mutual funds which are *open-end mutual funds*. We will discuss closed-end mutual funds later, as they are significantly different.

How a mutual fund works

As you can see from the previous discussion, deciding what stock or bond to buy with your money is a challenging task, especially for a new investor. Picking a common stock or corporate bond really means understanding and evaluating the company that issues the security. To build a broad portfolio, you will have to evaluate many companies. In evaluating a company, you are competing against professional stock analysts, as well as people who work in that industry or in that very company. These are people who have more investment training, more company knowledge, and more up-to-date information than you or I have. We are at a severe disadvantage and need help.

Mutual funds arose to answer this need. When you invest with a mutual fund, you hand your money over to a professional investment manager who will make investment decisions for you and the other mutual fund shareholders. Your money is pooled together with that of other investors to purchase stocks and bonds which are owned by the mutual fund. You own shares of the mutual fund. On your brokerage statement, you will see shares of the mutual fund listed, but you will not see listed the individual stocks and bonds held within the mutual fund. You can find a list of the fund's holdings in its semiannual and annual shareholder reports, where the manager discusses the mutual fund's investment strategy. However, the list of holdings will have changed by the time you receive the report.

Shares of open-end mutual funds are sold by the mutual fund company directly to the public or through distributing brokers. You can open an account at the mutual fund company or at a brokerage to buy shares. When you sell your mutual fund shares, you sell them back to the mutual fund company. When you place an order, your order and all other orders are transacted once a day overnight. Mutual fund shares are not traded during market hours on the exchanges the way individual stocks are actively traded. While stock and bond prices fluctuate during the trading session, the open-end mutual fund share price does not.

The share price of the mutual fund is determined once a day after the close of the market. The mutual fund's total *net asset value* (NAV) is compiled from the closing price of each individual stock and bond as well as the cash held in the mutual fund. The share price is equal to the net asset value per share. For U.S. stocks, the market close is 4:00 pm New York City time. The mutual fund price, when quoted during the trading day, is as of the close of market the previous trading day. When quoted later in the evening, the fund price may be updated as of that day's market close.

When you place an order to buy or sell a mutual fund, your order will be transacted at the next close of market share price. The determination of that price could be hours away. An order placed after market close on Friday will be executed at the close of market price on Monday. In the meantime the market could move significantly, and you will not know your trade price until after the transaction occurs.

This limited trading in mutual funds is consistent with the idea that you hand your money over to a professional to manage and trade for you. In choosing to invest with a mutual fund, you are implementing a long-term buy-and-hold strategy with the fund. The mutual fund will actively trade stocks or bonds, but the mutual fund itself is not meant to be traded like stocks. Some funds will charge an early redemption fee if you sell the fund too soon, say within 90 days of purchase.

Mutual fund manager

A mutual fund is run by the portfolio manager. This may be an individual or a team of managers. They in turn are supported by a staff of stock or bond analysts. In buying a mutual fund, you hire the manager to make your stock or bond decisions for you. You should evaluate the portfolio manager and analysts on their long-term performance track record over a period of at least five years to ten years or more.

The mutual fund manager usually works directly for the mutual fund company that offers her fund, though that is not always the case. Some mutual fund investment companies will develop their own in-house portfolio managers and research analysts to run their mutual funds. Other companies that sponsor mutual funds, such as a bank or an insurance company, may contract with outside third-party managers to run mutual funds under the sponsor's brand name, instead of hiring their own fund managers. The third-party managers may also offer mutual funds under their own name. A sought-after portfolio manager could be managing several almost identical mutual funds for different mutual fund companies. This means you could hire that same manager via several different brand name mutual funds, so you could look for her services at the mutual fund with the lowest expenses.

We will discuss further how to select managers and buy mutual funds in a later section.

Mutual fund styles

Mutual funds tend to have specific *investment styles*. The investment style derives from the investment philosophy of the portfolio manager and from the set of companies assigned to them to focus on. The fund's portfolio manager and analysts try to develop superior expertise in the companies they research. A mutual fund company may offer many different mutual funds with various styles. The mutual fund prospectus will describe the investment style and philosophy of the portfolio manager and the analysts. You should carefully read the fund's prospectus and latest annual report before investing in any mutual fund to understand how your money will be invested. The selling agent should give you the mutual fund prospectus, and both the prospectus and annual report should be available online at the mutual fund's website.

Investment styles become particularly important when we discuss how to implement your mutual fund strategy and your portfolio asset allocation in the chapters on investment strategy.

Among stock mutual funds a major style is the U.S. domestic large-cap stock fund, where "cap" is short for capitalization, which refers to the total dollar value of all the outstanding stock of a company. Almost all the companies that are household names are large-cap stocks: McDonald's, Johnson & Johnson, Wells Fargo & Co., Apple, Home Depot, Verizon Communications, Walt Disney Co., Ford Motor Co., and so forth. All of the stocks of the S&P 500 are U.S. large-cap domestic companies. Similarly, there are the mid-cap and small-cap styles based on the size of the company. Most mid-cap and small-cap stocks tend to be unfamiliar names to the pubic at large. Some funds don't specialize by size and invest with an all-cap style.

Segmenting by company size can be rather arbitrary. Mutual funds have variously defined size by dollar capitalization, or by ranking the biggest 1,000 companies followed by the next 1,000 companies, or by simply the company's inclusion on some index stock list. The important thing is you must read the mutual fund's prospectus to see how that fund describes its own investment process.

Besides company size, the other major style division for stock mutual funds is between growth and value. Growth funds invest in companies that are growing their sales revenue and earnings rapidly. Value funds focus on companies perceived by the manager to be undervalued below their intrinsic value, perhaps due to new products introduced by a competitor or to an economic downturn. The manager believes the company will recover as will its stock price.

Stock mutual funds use many other investing styles. One cut at investing styles is by U.S. domestic companies versus foreign companies, so a mutual fund might invest in foreign small-cap stocks. Geographic funds invest in one country such as China or one region such as Europe. Sector funds invest in companies within one industrial sector, such as health-care, natural resources, retail, or technology. Dividend funds invest in dividend-paying stocks.

Bond mutual funds have their own set of styles. You will find municipal bond funds, U.S. treasury and agency bond funds, corporate bond funds, foreign bond funds, and high-yield (junk) bond funds.

Some mutual funds invest in both stocks and bonds. These blended style funds include balanced funds and income funds (with dividend-paying stocks and interest-paying bonds). The idea behind balanced funds is to provide greater investment safety through a broader diversification across both stocks and bonds, all in one fund. While you could replicate the blended style by buying separate stock and bond funds, the balanced fund provides the added service of rebalancing. The manager will buy and sell bonds or stocks to shift the balance between them as market conditions warrant. This rebalancing would be a chore for you as an individual selling and buying two separate stock and bond mutual funds, as well as determining when to do so.

Target date mutual funds are a variation of the balanced fund. These retirement-oriented funds have a target date, such as a 2045 fund or a 2060 fund, when you plan to begin withdrawals for income. As the retirement date draws nearer, the fund will adjust the balance from stocks toward bonds. Their idea is that as you approach retirement you need the greater safety of bonds for your retirement assets. Target date funds require a long-term buy-and-hold strategy.

Stock mutual fund

A large equity mutual fund with billions of investor dollars will invest in hundreds of different companies. In doing so, the fund lowers its overall risk, since any one company that it owns doing poorly will have a relatively small effect on the portfolio. Conversely, any one highly successful company will have a diluted benefit. The equity fund hopes to find more winners than losers among its stock selections.

Mutual funds constantly trade the stocks in their portfolio, as they continually reevaluate the changing outlook for their companies. While some winners may be held for years, nonperforming stocks can be quickly dumped. This stock turnover can be very high, and the portfolio *turnover ratio* gives a measure of this activity. The turnover ratio is the dollar value of shares sold during the past 12 months divided by the total net asset value (NAV) of the fund. A high turnover ratio, say, near or over 1.0, indicates more active trading by the manager with the accumulation of transaction costs. This adds to the mutual fund's expenses and reduces your return.

The turnover ratio also gives a clue to the effectiveness of the fund manager in choosing good companies to begin with, as a lower turnover means they are holding on to more of the companies they have selected. So when comparing mutual funds, one thing to look for is a lower turnover ratio, which indicates a more efficient and effective manager. The exception would be the manager with the trading skill to generate enough profit to overcome the hurdle of the higher trading costs.

Stock trading by the mutual fund manager will generate gains and losses within the fund. These stock trading gains and losses by the manager are separate from the gain or loss from your buying and selling shares of the mutual fund itself. Also, many stocks held in the mutual fund will pay dividends to the fund. The stock trading gains, when greater than the losses, plus the dividends will be distributed periodically by the mutual fund as cash to its shareholders. The share price of the mutual fund will drop on the day of the distribution to reflect the reduction in the NAV of the fund from the outgoing distributions.

As an alternative to receiving the cash, you can instead elect to have the distributions automatically reinvested in the fund. The mutual fund will then use the cash to purchase additional shares for you. Your account will then show an increase in the number of shares, while the share price drops. Your NAV will remain unchanged by the distribution, as the value of the new shares will equal the value of the distribution.

Reinvesting the distributions back into the mutual fund is a critical and necessary step in letting your investment grow through compound earnings. In the early accumulation years of your investment plan, you should never take the distributed cash and spend it, unless it is for your planned goal for that investment, such as retirement or college tuition. If you take and spend the distribution cash you will slow your climb up the compound earnings timeline and severely limit your future purchasing power.

Bond mutual fund

Much of what we discussed about stock mutual funds also applies to bond mutual funds: They invest in hundreds of bonds for safety through diversification. They make periodic distributions from interest earned and net capital gains less losses. They allow automatic reinvestment of distributions. A lower turnover ratio indicates greater efficiency and effectiveness of the manager.

You will find that bond mutual funds invest in a range of bond quality from AAA to junk bonds. The most conservative bond funds will invest only in U.S. treasuries, the safest security. Others funds will focus on investment grade corporate bonds. Some funds will try to boost their returns by adding a small allotment of selected junk bonds with higher yields. Bond funds buy and sell bonds in massive volume to minimize their transaction costs. Their yields and capital gains and losses are driven by changes in the prevailing interest rates.

Investing in bonds through a mutual fund involves a different type of risk than buying and owning diverse individual bonds yourself, if you could afford it. The key difference is that individual bonds mature on a specific date, while bond mutual funds do not. Any bond you personally own will mature and pay back to you par value, so you have the chance to avoid an unrealized capital loss by waiting it out. However, a bond mutual fund never matures, and on no specific date can you expect to collect your initial invested amount. You have to sell your mutual fund shares, redeeming them at whatever the NAV is on the sale date, realizing a capital gain or loss. So when prevailing interest rates go up, the bonds held by the bond mutual fund will go down in value taking the NAV and fund share price down with them. Though individual bonds in the mutual fund may mature and repay par to the fund, all the fund's bonds will never mature on the same day, so the fund NAV as a whole will remain depressed.

Another source of risk with bond mutual funds is from the active trading of bonds by the fund managers. In their competitive world, aggressive bond fund managers in an attempt to boost capital gains will trade bonds much like managers in a stock mutual fund will trade stocks. However, the buying and selling of bonds of can result in losses as much as gains and also incur additional transaction costs to the fund. Aggressive high-yield bond funds will trade junk bonds and are just as risky as, if not more risky than, stock funds.

As an individual, you would typically buy and hold bonds to maturity while collecting the regular interest payments for income or reinvestment. When the bond matures and pays you par, you would reinvest the cash into a new bond. There are bond funds that implement a similarly conservative strategy, buying and holding only high quality bonds, content with the steady interest income. You will have to read the bond fund's prospectus to see whether a fund is conservative or actively engaged in aggressive bond trading.

Mutual fund pros and cons

Mutual funds offer several major advantages to individual investors.

They provide access to a professional investment team that would otherwise be unaffordable to individual investors who are not immensely wealthy. Your money is invested by the mutual fund manager who selects the stocks and bonds in the portfolio. The fund manager is in turn supported by stock and bond analysts, who recommend the stocks and bonds. The analysts study companies as their full-time job, so they can develop expertise in particular companies or an industrial sector. Managers and analysts of large mutual funds have better access to company officers and information than individual investors. They attend special events sponsored by companies such as analyst days, new product introduction events, and quarterly teleconferences, where company executives will speak and answer questions from the analysts. Also, mutual fund companies exercise constant oversight of their funds and evaluate the portfolio managers and analysts, replacing underperformers.

Mutual funds reduce your investment risk through diversification, which is investing in many different companies, more than you as an individual could research and purchase. We will discuss diversification later as part of investment strategy. The basic idea is not to put all your eggs in one basket. You as an individual investor will find it impractical to study hundreds of different companies in order to find 30 to 60 promising stocks to invest in.

Mutual fund managers can develop specialize expertise. Examples are sector funds that only invest in companies in, for example, natural resources, financial institutions, retail, or technology. They may hire experts who have worked in those industries to be stock analysts. An analyst in a highly technical area such as bio-tech may need a PhD in that field.

Mutual funds lower your overall transaction costs. Mutual funds pool the money from many investors and trade in very large dollar volumes of stocks or bonds. Trading in large blocks reduces the transaction cost per share; you benefit from the mutual fund's trading and operational efficiency. You would find the sales commissions very costly when buying relatively few shares of many different companies.

However, mutual funds also have some counterbalancing disadvantages.

There is a real lack of transparency with mutual funds; you don't know what companies the managers currently have you invested in. The annual report will list the stock and bond holdings as of the report date, but that is a snapshot. By the time you receive the report, the report may be months old, and substantial changes to the stock or bond holdings will have occurred. A seriously misleading practice that some portfolio managers engage in is to dress up their portfolios at fiscal year end specifically for the annual report. They will sell their losers and buy recently winning stocks to showcase in the annual report. This will make their mutual fund appear better than how it actually performed.

Investors may or may not care about transparency if the mutual fund is performing well. However, some investors want to avoid investing in certain companies for ethical reasons. They want to shun tobacco companies, gambling casinos, military arms suppliers, alcoholic beverage companies, sugary drink companies, or purveyors of unhealthy foods. Other investors want to make a political statement with their investing by boycotting companies that do business in countries that discriminate against women, exacerbate global climate change with carbon emissions, or oppress their citizens. Ordinary mutual funds may not be the right investment vehicle for investors with strongly felt convictions. Some mutual fund companies have created the "ethical" or "socially responsible" investment style to serve the needs of these investors.

Another concern with mutual funds is that the actions of the other investors in the fund can adversely affect you. For example, if during an economic crisis some investors in the mutual fund panic and rush to redeem their shares, the managers may be forced to sell stocks or bonds at a depressed price. The managers may prefer to wait out the crisis but are forced to sell the most liquid stocks and bonds to raise money to pay to the investors selling their shares back to the mutual fund. This will cause added transaction costs for the fund as well as reduce the number of shareholders. The burden of the fund expenses will be spread across a smaller number of shares and raise your per share expenses. The manager may have to sell some stocks that she wanted to keep, weakening the potential for the fund to recover after the crisis passes.

Mutual fund tax quirks

A major complaint about mutual funds centers on the unpredictable nature of distributions and how they can play havoc with income tax planning. Most mutual funds make their capital gain and dividend distributions usually in the last two months of the year, though funds can make distributions throughout the year. When the distributions occur near the end of the year, it can be difficult to determine how to adjust your tax withholding with your employer to cover unknown potential distribution amounts. Unexpectedly large distributions at year-end could leave you owing additional income tax. You may need to make a last quarter estimated tax payment to the federal and state governments to avoid penalties. Consult your tax advisor regarding any need for estimated tax payments.

Another unpopular tax situation occurs when you receive a distribution shortly after you buy a mutual fund. You will have to pay tax on that distribution. For example, you invest $10,000 in a mutual fund on November 20, and on December 12 your new mutual fund pays a 10% distribution of $1,000. You will have to pay tax on that $1000 distribution in this tax year. This is true even if the value of the mutual fund is unchanged or if it has dropped and you have an unrealized loss on your recent purchase. People have found it frustrating to have to pay tax when they have no gain or even a loss on the new purchase. However, this situation is not quite as bad as it appears, since the NAV of your mutual fund shares is adjusted down $1,000 to reflect the distribution. The NAV adjustment down gives you an unrealized loss of $1,000 for a tax savings later when you sell the mutual fund, which will offset the tax paid this year on the $1,000 distribution.

Though you have to pay tax on that immediate distribution, you do not, as some people claim, "pay someone else's tax." You pay only the tax that you yourself owe. The mutual fund bookkeeping and the tax laws are sophisticated enough to keep it all straight. The real effect is on the timing of when you pay your tax, that being the early payment in the year of the distribution.

Index mutual fund

The index mutual fund is a style whose popularity has grown immensely. A market index uses a set of representative companies to track a specific market or sector. The well-known S&P 500 index tracks the aggregated price movements of 500 leading U.S. large-cap stocks. Most of the major mutual fund companies now offer their own version of an S&P 500 index fund. Today a plethora of indices tracks everything from the largest companies, to companies in narrow industrial sectors, to companies in foreign countries, to eclectic collections of faddish companies. Many index mutual funds have been created each based on some particular index. There are indices and mutual funds based on them to track companies in all the major stock styles, such as growth, value, large-cap, mid-cap, or small-cap styles. The name of the fund, and certainly the fund prospectus, will tell you which index it tracks.

Similarly, bond indices track various bond markets. However, bond index funds have not gained the same following as stock index funds. If you are considering a bond index fund just for its lower fund expenses versus a managed fund, you may be better off buying individual bonds directly in a bond ladder. We will discuss bond ladders in the chapter on investment strategies.

Market indices are created and published by private companies such as financial media companies, banks, and brokerages. The stocks that make up an index are selected by a committee at the publisher of the index. While the companies are nominally selected to be "representative" and not for stock price performance, the publishers know full well that a dynamic index filled with exciting companies will generate more interest than an index listing stagnant, old guard companies. When an index is updated, invariably an old fading company is replaced by a rising star. Indices have a bias toward successful companies.

The companies selected for an index essentially constitute a portfolio like any other. Publication editors and stock analysts select the companies in the index portfolio. There is nothing magical about the companies in an index that would give the index portfolio any advantage over any other portfolio. Any advantage that index mutual funds have comes entirely from their lower operating expenses.

The popularity of investing with index funds, of *index investing* as the practice is called, arises from the lower expenses that index funds enjoy compared to actively managed funds with the same investment style. Because the representative companies in an index have been pre-selected and rarely change, index funds do not incur the cost of a staff of analysts researching hundreds of companies. Index funds are passive and save on transaction costs due to their very low turnover ratio. This passive index investing results in cost savings that pass through to you in a higher NAV.

You must exercise some care in selecting an index fund. The index fund could replace dozens of individual companies in your portfolio. Though index funds are presumed to be diversified, they are only as diversified as is the underlying index. If you are interested in an index fund tracking a narrow sector dominated by a few companies, you should still look at those dominant companies to judge their overall quality. An index fund must fit into the investment strategy that you will develop in subsequent chapters.

Active management versus passive index fund

An ongoing debate in financial circles, and especially in the media, is whether a mutual fund actively managed by a portfolio manager and his team of analysts can deliver higher returns than a similarly styled passive index fund with its lower expenses. The higher expenses of the actively managed fund is a hurdle the fund manager must leap just to get even with the index fund. Various studies have confirmed that most large-cap fund managers over a period of years underperformed a passive S&P 500 index fund in net return. This raises the serious question of whether you should just invest with passive index funds rather than with actively managed funds.

Note that the valid comparison is between an actively managed fund and an index fund, not between an active fund and the index itself. Even an index fund has administrative expenses, while an index is purely a number. You will find that different index funds tracking the same index have varied in performance, and almost all index funds also have underperformed the pure index. Again, you must take care to choose a good index fund.

The active versus passive argument has ardent believers on both sides, so much so that it has become almost a religious argument. Neither side will ever convince the other. Nonetheless, with that background story, I will briefly give my point of view, and then we will move on.

The performance of a pure index, which is designed to represent its market sector, should represent the aggregated performance of all the investors in its market. If we were to grade an index fund together with all the actively managed funds on a curve, like in school, we can reasonably presume that the gross performance, before expenses, of any index mutual fund would be near the mean or average. However, since the index fund has an advantage of lower operating costs, its net performance will be better than average. So let's raise its net performance grade from an average 50% up to, say, 60% or even 80%. This is roughly the range of results reported in various comparative studies, that the index fund beats 60% to 80% of active fund managers. This is comparable to raising the index fund's grade from a "C" to a "B."

What does this tell us? Yes, an index fund with its lower expense advantage will likely beat most active managers. Nevertheless, like grading on a curve, the top 20% of active managers over some period of years will beat an index fund. These are the grade "A" managers. The task in hiring a mutual fund manager is to find those top 20% of long-term higher performing managers. The "A" managers are definitely out there.

From another perspective, choosing a mutual fund manager is really a hiring decision. You know from your experience at work, as a manager or an employee, that employees vary greatly in their talent and contributions. Top employees deliver results over and over. The same thing applies to portfolio managers. You want to hire that talented, top contributing portfolio manager. Talent ultimately rises to the top.

So, you have some choices. You can passively invest with an index fund and most likely get above average returns—which is a perfectly fine strategy. Or, you can find and hire a fund manager whose track record shows he can deliver top tier returns, albeit with a bit more volatility. Finally, you could blend strategies by putting some money into an index fund and some money into a managed fund. We will discuss how to find and hire mutual fund managers, as well as discuss mutual fund strategies, in later chapters.

Mutual fund fees

We will discuss an overall fee structure for your portfolio in a later chapter. The purpose here is to prepare you for a mutual fund fee discussion with your financial advisor or the mutual fund company representative. Mutual fund sales charges, fees, and expenses come in several moving parts, and the details vary greatly depending on the specific mutual fund you are considering. You will need to ask your financial advisor many questions to gain a sufficient understanding of the mutual fund fees. You should expect him to take the time to explain patiently share classes and the associated sales loads and ongoing expenses and fees, so you can choose the share class with the lowest cost to you.

(At this point, I suggest that you look up online the prospectus of a mutual fund with a sales load in order to follow along in this discussion.)

The *sales load* is a sales commission paid by the mutual fund company to the financial advisor who helps you choose and then sells the fund to you. So, if you invest $10,000 in a mutual fund with a 5% load, a sales commission of $500 goes to your financial advisor, and $9,500 goes into the mutual fund as your NAV. The *share class* determines when this sales charge will be collected from you. With Class A shares you pay the load at the front-end at the time of purchase. The Class A sales load can be reduced (as a percentage) when you invest larger amounts exceeding certain thresholds known as *breakpoints*. With Class B shares you pay the sales load at the back-end when you sell the shares. As you hold B shares over a number of years, the back-end sales load percentage declines yearly until it reaches zero. Then the B shares convert to A shares, and you will not have to pay the back-end sales load nor the front-end sales load if you had bought A shares to begin with. Class C shares don't have any sales commission as such.

A mutual fund also charges you ongoing fees to cover their operating expenses. The fees are deducted from investment returns and reduce the NAV. In a mutual fund's prospectus you will find a table listing the fund's annual expenses as a percentage of the NAV, which is your total invested amount. These fund expenses include management fees, administrative fees, other expenses, and distribution and service fees. The key line in the table to look at is the "Total annual fund operating expenses." You will see that the total operating expense ratio varies with the share class, and that the A shares have lower operating expenses than B or C shares. The A, B, and C shares have different expenses primarily due to their different 12b-1 fees.

The 12b-1 fees are distribution and service fees paid quarterly to the brokerage that holds your mutual fund shares to help offset their costs. In practice the 12b-1 fee goes to your financial advisor as part of his compensation. The B shares have a higher 12b-1 fee to offset the decline in the back-end sales load each year. Similarly, for C shares, which have no sales load, the higher 12b-1 fee replaces the sales commission for the financial advisor.

For buy-and-hold investors, Class A shares with their low ongoing expense ratio after a number of years will cost you less in total than B or C shares. Class B shares appeal to those buyers who do not want to pay a front-end sales load. They agree to a higher total expense ratio and plan to hold the mutual fund for a number of years until the shares convert to A shares, when the back-end sales load is waived and the expense ratio drops. Class C shares appeal to people who don't want to pay any sales load and only plan to hold the mutual fund for a short few years, say three to four years. Since their expense ratio never drops, C shares over time eventually become more expensive than A or B shares. Class C shares become disadvantageous when a planned short-term hold extends into a long-term hold.

When you purchase a mutual fund, you should ask your financial advisor or the mutual fund sales person the following questions:

- What is the front-end or back-end sales load? (Typically, 4%-5%)
- When do the Class B share convert to Class A shares? How much does the expense ratio drop then?
- Is there a *contingent deferred sales charge* (CDSC)? How does it work?

- Why are you recommending Class C shares (when Class A shares are cheaper for a buy-and-hold strategy)?
- Is there an *early redemption fee*? When is it charged?
- Can I save money with *breakpoints*? (A lower sales load for larger invested amounts)
- Can I save money with a *Letter of Intent*? (A lower sales load for larger amounts invested over time)
- Ask to see the *sales charge and expense tables* in the prospectus. Ask him to explain it to you.
- Is there any transaction fee, in addition to the sales load, on buying the mutual fund?

Pursuing these questions will help you buy the right class of shares for your investment needs. Don't be afraid to ask any and all your questions.

In a later section we will discuss additional mutual fund share classes that are available only in 401(k) and fee-based investment accounts.

No-load mutual fund

As competition in the burgeoning mutual fund industry intensified, some mutual fund companies began competing for customers on sales price by eliminating sales charges. They introduced *no-load* mutual funds that do not charge a sales load. With a no-load mutual fund all of your $10,000 investment is invested for you, so your starting NAV is the full $10,000. Purchasing no-load funds offers you a significant cost savings over sales loaded funds. No-load funds do charge ongoing expense fees to cover their operating costs. No-load funds can charge a 12b-1 fee, though many do not. Note that the brokerage may charge a transaction fee on no-load fund trades.

Eliminating the sales load means that commissioned financial advisors are not paid for selling no-load mutual funds. Consequently, no-load mutual funds are primarily sold through discount brokerages or directly by the mutual fund company. Since there is no sales commission for a financial advisor, they can only use no-load funds in a fee-based managed account. Fee-based accounts replace sales charges with an annual management fee that is a fixed percentage of the assets under management including no-load funds. We will discuss managed investment accounts later under investment strategies.

In competing on low price, do no-load funds offer lower performance? Do mutual funds with sales loads have better portfolio managers? In my reviewing the performance of many mutual funds over the years, there seems to be no difference. The best performing mutual fund mangers are found in both loaded and no-load mutual funds. Charging a sales load does not imply those fund managers are better performers with superior results. In fact, the sales load must be added to the fund's expenses as an even greater hurdle for the fund managers to jump in competing with no-load index funds. If the portfolio management teams are equally talented, and all else being equal, the no-load fund with its lower fees is preferable.

So when would you choose a no-load mutual fund and when would you ever choose a sales loaded mutual fund? I will give you three basic rules of guidance in choosing a sales loaded fund versus a no-load fund.

First, compare the long-term track record of net performance of the mutual funds, where the returns are based on the full purchase price including any sales load, and not based on the beginning NAV where the sales load has been subtracted. The loaded fund will need ongoing higher net performance to catch up to or surpass the no-load fund. This ultimately comes down to your hiring decision of the better portfolio management team.

Second, if your relationship with your financial advisor is commission-based (as opposed to fee-based), and you feel that his advice is worth paying for, then you might consider the sales load as payment for his advice. After paying your financial advisor, you would then use the reduced beginning NAV to calculate and compare the performance of the mutual funds.

Third, don't buy a passive index fund with a sales load. Here finding management talent is not a factor, and only the lower fund expenses matter.

Exchange-traded fund

The exchange-traded fund (ETF) gives you an alternative to the index mutual fund. In the past few decades ETFs have grown in popularity to rival index mutual funds. Whether you choose an index ETF or an index mutual fund will depend on your investment strategy. Note that the previous discussion comparing passive index funds to actively managed mutual funds also applies to passive ETFs versus actively managed mutual funds.

An equity ETF generally holds all of the stocks in the index it tracks and provides you diversification across those securities. You own shares of the exchange-traded fund, and your shares represent an interest in each stock in the index. An ETF is passive, since it simply holds the specific securities in the index and does not trade them. ETFs are transparent in that you are able to see the list of every stock currently held in the ETF. ETFs are a useful tool for you to invest broadly in a market sector, for example transportation or healthcare, at a lower transaction cost compared to buying a selection of the individual stocks in the sector. ETFs have been created to track virtually any market index or sector you care to buy.

ETFs are marketed by sponsoring companies whose brand names you may recognize. Two examples of famous ETFs include SPY which tracks the S&P 500 index. The ticker symbol SPY refers to an ETF from the SPDR (nicknamed "spider") family of ETFs tracking various indices. Another famous ETF, with the symbol QQQ, is the PowerShares QQQ ETF, which tracks the NASDAQ 100 Index. The PowerShares QQQ is heavily tech oriented, mirroring the NASDAQ 100. You will find many other families of ETFs as you study ETF investing.

The ETF sponsors work with partners known as *authorized participants*, which are large financial institutions such as banks and investment companies, to create and redeem the ETF shares issued onto the exchanges.

With so many investment companies offering ETFs, a major index like the S&P 500 will have many ETFs tracking it. If you buy an S&P 500 ETF, be careful to study and understand what you are buying. Even something as seemingly straightforward as an S&P 500 ETF can be misunderstood, because some ETFs will have their own spin on how they track that index. For example, the S&P 500 index is a market-value weighted index, which means the stock price movements of the most valuable companies in the index, such as Apple or Exxon Mobil, have a greater effect on the index than price movements of smaller companies. A true S&P 500 ETF will also be market-value weighted. To differentiate itself, a variant S&P 500 ETF may place equal weight on all the companies in the index, which means the price movements of smaller companies will have as great an effect as larger companies, magnifying the importance of the smaller companies in that ETF compared to the S&P 500 index. An equal-weighted S&P 500 ETF will perform differently than a market-weighted S&P 500 ETF.

ETFs are also available to track bond sectors such as intermediate-term bonds or long-term bonds. You must take some care in choosing a bond ETF that follows a bond index. Because the federal government issues overwhelmingly more bond debt than any other domestic issuer, a bond index can be heavily overweighted with U.S. government bonds. You may want to diversify your bonds by adding ETFs that exclude government bonds, such as an ETF of intermediate-term corporate bonds. Study each ETF's list of holdings so you understand the underlying bonds and how much of each bond you are buying. Like a bond mutual fund, a bond ETF does not have a maturity date as an individual bond does. On its maturity date, an individual bond repays its par value. See the previous discussion of bond mutual funds regarding the added risk from not having a maturity date. The same risk is present with bond ETFs.

ETF or index mutual fund

In choosing between ETFs and index mutual funds you need to consider how they fit in your overall investment strategy and how you go about investing. We will have a complete discussion of investment strategy in later chapters. Here we will highlight the relative advantage of ETFs or index mutual funds for different investment needs you may have.

Lower operating expenses give ETFs an advantage over index mutual funds. ETFs have lower expense ratios because their sponsors have no shareholder bookkeeping costs, no shareholder transaction costs, no client or financial advisor service call centers, less management overhead, and no costs for annual reports to shareholders. Where ETFs can be purchased without a sales commission, such as in a fee-based account, they have an advantage with their lower expense hurdle toward providing higher returns than index mutual funds. For long-term buy-and-hold investors the cost savings can accumulate significantly.

Where you do incur the sales commission for purchasing ETFs, you need to consider the mode of your saving and investing. If you will be saving regularly over the years toward retirement, you will be making frequent investment purchases, typically monthly or quarterly. Perhaps, you might set up a payroll deduction to be sent to your brokerage for periodic investment. When you make many purchases in relatively small amounts, say under $1,000 per purchase, you will want to avoid sales commissions with each purchase that will add up over time to a large expense. With ETFs you will accumulate commission costs over time. No-load index funds have no sales cost for purchasing in small amounts. In this case, no-load funds work better for periodic small purchases.

Similarly, no-load funds work better for dollar cost averaging which also involves regular periodic purchases. More on dollar cost averaging later in investment strategies.

If you want flexibility to change strategies, no-load mutual funds allow you to change your funds cost effectively. You can switch from a no-load fund in one index/sector to another index/sector fund with no sales cost. With ETF's you would incur sales charges on the sale of one ETF and on the purchase of the new ETF, in a commission-based account.

As we discussed in a previous chapter, you will want to take full advantage of compounding earnings by reinvesting your dividend and capital gain distributions from your ETF or index mutual fund. For mutual funds you can can set up automatic reinvestment of your distributions with the mutual fund company to compound your earnings. Mutual funds do not charge a fee for reinvesting distributions. In the case of ETFs you will need to set up a reinvestment plan for distributions with your financial advisor or broker, if they offer that service. Before you purchase an ETF from any broker, be sure to ask if they offer automatic reinvestment of ETF distributions, how it works, and what the cost will be to you, as they might charge a sales commission for reinvesting distributions. You cannot forgo reinvesting your distributions, so find a broker who provides reinvestment services, at no cost if possible. Some brokers do offer free reinvestment services.

Trading ETFs

An ETF behaves like a hybrid of stock and index mutual fund. An ETF offers the diversification of a mutual fund holding a portfolio of stocks, while it can trade with the frequency of stocks. You as an individual would buy exchange-traded fund shares on the stock exchange through your broker. Purchasing or selling an ETF will incur a sales commission like trading a stock. Unlike an index mutual fund which trades once a day after the close of the market when its NAV is determined, an ETF's price fluctuates throughout the trading day just like stock prices. Due to the action of market supply and demand, the ETF can trade at a spot price above or below the NAV of its component companies; however, arbitrage trading by institutional traders usually keeps the spot price discount or premium to a narrow range close to the NAV. (Arbitrage trading occurs whenever a significant price discrepancy appears. Institutional traders will buy or sell the ETF, while simultaneously making the opposite trade by selling or buying all the component stocks, to pocket the price difference. This is possible because the institution can purchase or redeem ETF shares directly with the ETF issuer at the NAV of the underlying shares.)

As we have discussed and will repeat often, investing is a long-term activity. Both ETFs and mutual funds can fit well into your long-term investment strategy. Mutual funds are designed to encourage holding them for the long term. On the other hand, ETFs trade on exchanges along with stocks, and the temptation is always there to treat them like stocks, for example checking on their prices during the day's trading session.

If you have a trading account which is your separate hobby account, you can include ETFs in among the stocks that you trade. Because ETFs hold all the stocks of their indices, they offer immediate diversification for the same amount of money as you might invest in one stock. In general, a single stock can crater with a bad earnings report or soar with great earnings. An ETF will reflect the aggregated performance of all its component stocks, some good, some bad, all averaging somewhere in the middle. Trading with diversified ETFs can be safer than trying to pick individual stocks.

Styles of ETF

ETFs have proven so popular with investors that the companies that issue them rapidly expanded beyond basic ETFs tracking indices. In order to attract more of your investment dollars away from mutual funds, sponsors have introduced ETFs that mirror the styles and strategies of mutual funds, for example dividend ETFs, growth ETFs, multi-asset allocation ETFs, target date ETFs, and real estate ETFs. Review the previous discussion of styles of mutual funds, which applies just as well to styles of ETFs.

Styled ETFs have portfolios comparable to similarly styled mutual funds. The ETF portfolio is initially chosen by the analysts at the sponsoring company or the index publisher. Thereafter, the ETF is passive, while the mutual fund is actively managed.

Counterintuitively, some of these new styles of ETF are actively managed, negating one of the primary cost advantages of ETFs in the first place. A note of caution is warranted regarding actively managed ETFs: They lack shareholder documentation. When you buy an ETF on the stock exchange, you do not get an ETF offering prospectus as you do with a mutual fund. The mutual fund prospectus explains its investment strategy, risks, and expenses. Without ETF annual reports it is harder to evaluate the performance of the ETF managers. Evaluating an actively managed ETF is completely different than evaluating a basic ETF that tracks an index you can directly compare it to. An actively managed ETF should be compared not only to some relevant index but also to other similarly styled ETFs and mutual funds.

Exotic ETF

Exotic ETFs come in many creative styles. They have incorporated investment techniques originally pioneered by hedge funds. Exotic ETF have styles along the lines of: long short, high dividend yield hedged, hedged equity, private equity, currency hedged, minimum volatility, high beta, alternative alpha, tactical yield, 2x leveraged, half hedged, commodity optimized, technology bear 2x, focused futures, and so on. What these styles all have in common is that the average investor has no clue what they mean or how the ETF would invest his money.

My advice to you is simply this: If you don't understand the investment, avoid it. Many exotic ETFs defy evaluation even by research analysts. Some exotic ETFs have a built-in, long-term money losing trend; they are only usable as a short-term trade when you anticipate a specific triggering event. Instead of an exotic ETF, stick with a basic ETF that tracks a major market index that you understand.

Other investment types

Closed-end mutual fund

Despite its similar name, a *closed-end mutual fund* is very different from the open-end mutual fund that we have been discussing. In general, when people or the media talk about mutual funds they generally mean open-end mutual funds. Closed-end mutual funds are less well-known and less popular, however, they can serve a role in your portfolio. A closed-end fund can be useful in generating a retirement income stream.

A closed-end mutual fund consists of a portfolio of stocks and bonds actively managed by an investment company. With each common share, you own a portion of the closed-end fund which in turn owns the stocks and bonds in the portfolio. Closed-end funds offer professional management and diversification across its securities. Closed-end funds charge expense fees taken from investment returns.

Closed-end mutual fund common shares trade on the stock exchanges like stocks, so their prices fluctuate during the trading day, and you will incur a sales commission when you buy or sell. Unlike an ETF or open-end mutual fund, the number of common shares of the closed-end mutual fund is fixed. Once a closed-end fund is established and trades on the exchange, the fund does not issue new common shares or redeem shares.

A closed-end mutual fund may also issue preferred shares which are a debt security for borrowing money. The preferred shares pay a dividend, analogous to the interest paid by a bond. Preferred shares do not participate in the net gains or losses of the fund's portfolio.

Closed-end fund common shares often trade at a discount to NAV; the reasons are not well understood. Before you buy any closed-end mutual fund, you should find out the extent of any discount at which it commonly trades. The price of a closed-end mutual fund can fluctuate significantly below the NAV of its portfolio, at times dipping below a 15% discount. You would look to buy any closed-end fund at a price below its usual discount.

Never buy a closed-end mutual fund at a premium, because you would be paying more than the NAV, more than what the portfolio is worth. You may hear as a justification that the closed-end fund's talented management team is earning the premium. However, the closed-end fund's premium could easily fluctuate down to a discount, whereby you would suffer an unrealized loss. You would be better off buying into an equally talented management team at an open-end mutual fund at NAV with no premium.

One key feature distinguishes closed-end mutual funds from ETFs or open-end mutual funds: leverage, which comes from the ability to borrow money to invest. Because a closed-end mutual fund does not redeem its common shares, it is not vulnerable to client redemptions during a market downturn. The fund's asset base is relatively stable, which allows it to borrow money through issuing preferred shares. In a leveraged strategy, the portfolio manager uses the securities in the fund's portfolio as collateral to borrow, say, an additional 35% of the NAV. The manager will then invest this additional money, putting to work 135% of the NAV value before the borrowing. The idea is to borrow money at a lower cost (the dividends on the preferred shares) and invest it at a higher rate of return. This multiplies or leverages any potential gain or loss going to the common shares, with correspondingly more risk. With a stock portfolio which by nature is volatile, leverage is a very risky strategy that I would avoid. With a bond portfolio which is usually less volatile, this leverage risk can be managed by the professional mangers at the closed-end fund; nonetheless, bond portfolios leveraged with debt are inherently riskier. For some closed-end funds, the higher, leveraged return may appear to justify a premium, but the higher risk from the debt leverage offsets any higher return.

Many income-oriented closed-end mutual funds use leverage to enhance their return. When your objective is generating income, such an income fund could find a place in your portfolio. This is especially so, if you are able to purchase the closed-end fund at a discount price even below its usual discount. Then you get the dual benefit of the purchase discount plus the leverage provided by the management team. Remember that the price of an income-oriented closed-end fund will be sensitive to changes in the prevailing interest rates, similarly to bonds. See the previous discussion on bond prices and interest rates moving in opposite directions.

However, a caution, you must beware of the closed-end fund trap. When an income closed-end mutual fund establishes a record of paying high dividends on its common shares, its managers may be loathe to pay less even when the earnings on its portfolio can no longer support the high dividends. A dividend cut is extremely bad news to retirement shareholders who need the money to live on. In that case, the fund may choose to continue paying the high dividend with the hope that its earnings will recover. So long as this overpayment on the dividend continues, the fund is paying out all its earnings and making up the difference by returning part of the shareholder's principal investment as part of the dividend. Your NAV will fall. If you are unaware of this return of your principal and you spend the dividend, you will unknowingly spend down your retirement savings. You could prematurely run out of money. One way to monitor this potential trap is to look at the value of the closed-end fund on your brokerage statement—is it dropping more than the market? Another way is to look at the unrealized gain or loss for this closed-end fund on your brokerage statement. Any return of principal will reduce the value of your investment and appear as a drop in the unrealized gain or increase in the unrealized loss for your closed-end mutual fund. Ask your financial advisor to help you understand this potential trap.

Unit investment trust

The *unit investment trust* (UIT) is a portfolio of preselected stocks, bonds, or other securities that you purchase as a package, the unit. With a UIT you can know exactly what securities are in your unit, as they are listed in the prospectus. These securities stay fixed for the life of the UIT, which commonly is fixed at a year but can be set much longer depending on the strategy. The sponsoring investment company selects the securities seeking to offer a focused strategy that you as the UIT buyer believe is timely and will produce a gain over the period of the UIT. For example, you may feel that European stocks are overdue for a recovery, because European economies have been doing well. You can then buy a UIT focused on European stocks. There are myriad UIT strategies to chose from. The UIT may feature selected dividend appreciation stocks, tax-exempt municipal bonds, foreign stocks, or "undervalued" stocks.

You purchase the units of a UIT through your broker, with a sales charge. Other than at the initial selection of the securities, the UIT is not actively managed during its life. As a consequence, UITs charge all their expense fees up front with the sales charge. After issuance, the sponsor of a UIT may choose to buy and sell the UIT on the secondary market to provide investors some liquidity, but the sponsor is not required to do so. So you may not be able to sell prior to maturity. If you are able to sell, you may not receive the full NAV considering the sales charge. You should be prepared to hold the UIT to maturity as they are designed for. Upon maturity, the UIT is automatically liquidated and the proceeds distributed, though in some cases you can elect to receive the securities in the UIT instead of cash. The proceeds will be net of any gain or loss from your initial investment. At maturity, the sponsor often will revise the security selections and reissue the UIT. You can choose to roll your cash into the updated UIT, typically with a reduced sales charge for a renewal.

Because of its short life and the recurring sales charge to roll over the UIT, I believe they are best suited to pursuing a short-term tactical opportunity during the limited life of the UIT. For the long-term, buy-and-hold investor, a UIT's recurring sales charge compares unfavorably to the one-time sales cost of ETFs and mutual funds.

Real estate investment trust

The *real estate investment trust* (REIT) is an investment company that specializes in real estate, which is land and buildings. You buy shares of the REIT which in turn invests in land and buildings for apartments, shopping centers, hospitals, office buildings, hotels, or other types of real estate intensive business, including even timber land and cell phone towers. A REIT allows you to invest in real estate with a smaller amount of money than the price of a house or retail store building. It allows you to diversify your money across many different real estate properties. Also, a REIT can complement mutual funds or ETFs by further diversifying your portfolio beyond stocks and bonds into real estate.

The *equity REIT* owns real estate properties and rents them to tenants or business occupants. The REIT provides professional management of those properties. A REIT provides geographical diversity so that your real estate holdings are not overconcentrated in one city or region. Many REITs specialize in one type of real estate property. For example, a restaurant chain may want to spend its limited financial resources on growing its business by opening new restaurants. One way to make its money go farther is to rent the buildings from a REIT, which partners with the restaurant chain. The REIT uses its money to obtain or construct buildings to match the restaurant chain's floor plan. The restaurant focuses on serving food, while the REIT focuses on operating the real estate. The equity REIT's income is derived from rents, along with the gains from the sale of real estate. Also, the individual properties held in the REIT can appreciate in value, which results in an increase in the REIT share price.

Owning shares in an equity REIT is very different than owning rental real estate yourself. Since the REIT is a security traded on exchanges through your broker or financial advisor, it provides immediate liquidity, compared to the time needed to sell real estate. If you own rental property directly, you take on the risks of being in the rental business, for example you would need fire and liability insurance. You, as the landlord, or your hired property manager would manage the property and be responsible for repairs or settling disputes with the tenants.

Less common is the *mortgage REIT* which invests in the mortgages on properties. The mortgage REIT derives its income from the interest on the mortgages. Because it owns mortgage debt, as opposed to equity, the mortgage REIT behaves similarly to a bond portfolio in many ways. The mortgage REIT share price will be react inversely to prevailing interest rates changes. (See the previous discussion of bond prices and interest rates moving in opposite directions.) The share price of the mortgage REIT will not benefit from the appreciate of the underlying real estate properties.

A REIT can be very tax efficient for shareholders. When the REIT meets certain IRS rules, mainly that it distributes at least 90% of its income to shareholders, then the REIT itself is not taxed on the income that it distributes. After the distribution, the REIT shareholder is then taxed on the dividend she receives. The REIT dividend avoids the double taxation on stock dividends, where a company is taxed on its income first, and then after distribution the stockholder is taxed again on the dividend she receives. As a result, REITs pay a high dividend to shareholders. A high yielding REIT can complement dividend-paying stocks and bonds in an income portfolio. There are potential complexities to the taxation of your REIT income, so you may want to consult your tax advisor before investing.

Master limited partnership

As an investment, the *master limited partnership* (MLP) is all about income and cash flow. A MLP consists of many *limited partners*, who are the investors, and a *general partner*, who manages the investments and controls the partnership. Most MLPs invest in energy industry infrastructure, notably oil and gas pipelines. In 1987 when Congress limited the proliferation of MLPs, it specifically exempted the energy sector, preserving the MLP's pass-through tax advantages for that sector. The income from a pipeline is essentially a toll on the flow of oil or gas passing through it. Since energy drives the U.S. economy, the income from the distribution of oil and gas through pipelines is steady and predictable. Income investors look to the MLP as a tax-advantaged income alternative to corporate bonds, dividend-paying stocks, and REITs.

The limited partners supply investment capital to the MLP and own common units of the MLP. Limited partnership common units are traded on the exchanges through your broker. The limited partners receive regular cash distributions from their MLP units. The cash distribution to the limited partners is not taxed at the MLP level but is passed through to the limited partners. The limited partners are then taxed on the distribution on their individual tax returns. This pass-through avoids the double taxation on corporate dividends. The MLP's high cash flow and the pass-through tax efficiency appeal to income-oriented investors.

The general partner has complicated interests in the MLP. The general partner operates the pipelines, storage tanks, and other facilities of the MLP. For this management role, the general partner collects a fee. The general partner owns a general-partnership interest in the MLP, typically 2%, The general partner also retains the unsold limited partnership units. Generally, these unsold units are subordinate units to the common units sold to limited partners. The common units must first receive some minimum quarterly distribution amount, before any remaining income is distributed to the common units and the subordinate units.

As a potential MLP investor, you should evaluate the MLP mainly on its cash distributions. Evaluate it as an income complement to the bonds in your portfolio. However, the tax treatment for MLPs is complex and very different than for bonds or REITs. Before you invest in a MLP, you should consult with your tax advisor about how the pass-through of MLP income and deductions will affect your individual tax return, now and in the future.

A note of caution, in addition to the MLP itself as an investable entity, the general partner is a separate business entity, which may have shares of common stock of its own on the exchanges. To invest in the MLP look for the common units of the MLP for limited partners. If you go to buy an MLP, ask your a financial advisor or broker to verify you are buying the common units for the limited partners, and not the stock of the general partner, which may have a similar sounding name.

Structured product

The *structured product* is fundamentally a promissory note issued by a financial institution. With a structured note, you own a promise from the issuer of repayment of the principal plus or minus a calculated gain or loss at maturity, which can be one to ten years. The gain or loss is calculated based on the performance of an identified reference stock or index. You do not own any equity in the underlying stock or index, only debt from the issuing company. Structured products are sold through brokers. The issuer or your broker may offer to buy back the notes to provide some liquidity, but they are not required to do so nor to offer the entire calculated value of the structured product. You should plan on holding the structured product until maturity, with no early access to your invested funds.

The structured note's return profile is constructed from the performance of the reference stock or index. This calculation of the return can be simple, or it can be extremely complicated and completely recast the performance of the underlying reference stock or index. For example, some structured notes offer limited downside protection, say, a 10% safety buffer if the reference stock price were to have fallen upon maturity. So you would get your entire principal back if the stock fell no more than 10%, or suffer only a 3% loss if the stock fell 13%. A structured product can be constructed to offer a leveraged return, say, 120% of the actual index performance, be it a gain or a loss. Other structured products offer complex return profiles that mix buffers with return multipliers. A structured note can even offer reversed performance where the note gains when the index falls.

Structured product returns can be constructed ranging from very conservative with lesser risk to very aggressive with lots of risk. Structured products involve a lockup period tying up your money for years. Their complex return profiles can be very difficult to evaluate. You must also evaluate separately the creditworthiness of the issuing company. So, consult with your financial advisor before investing in a structured product.

Alternative investment

The *alternative investment* (AI) comprises a group of investments targeted to financial institutions and wealthy individuals. You will need to meet specific regulatory qualifications before you can be presented with an alternative investment or allowed to invest in it. This is because AIs often involve high risk, high fees, and high, unclear, potential reward. AIs are usually illiquid, you cannot expect to get your money out for one to five years or more. These AIs are purposely designed as lockup investments to allow the strategy time to work.

AIs can be very difficult to evaluate. It may not be possible to determine your actual return until after the lockup period ends. Often the AI has no track record to judge by. Many times the sales presentation is based solely on the reputation of the offering company and stresses the success of previous investment pools run by that company. Also, the effect on your tax situation can be complicated and last for many years.

You should seek the advice of your financial advisor and your tax accountant to help evaluate the pros and cons of any potential alternative investment.

Accredited investor

How do you know if you are an *accredited investor* to invest in a given alternative investment? First, most important, if you don't feel that you are a wealthy and sophisticated investor, then likely you aren't and perhaps should avoid the complexity and risk of alternative investments. Second, the sales representative should verify you meet the investor requirements, and the AI prospectus should list them as well.

Securities and Exchange Commission (SEC) rules define the accredited investor: Do you have, not including your primary residence, a net worth of at least $1,000,000; or do you have annual income of at least $200,000 individually (or $300,000 jointly with a spouse) for the past two years and likely for this current year as well? Then you are an accredited investor for alternative investments.

The purpose of qualifying investors is to protect innocent investors. The stocks, corporate bonds, mutual funds and other SEC registered investments offered to ordinary investors must abide by SEC regulations. AIs operate as unregistered investments to avoid much of the SEC restrictions. AIs also do not trade on the exchanges, so they are not bound by exchange rules. Hence, investors in AI's do not have these regulatory protections. Accredited investors, having wealth or high income, are presumed to have commensurate sophistication to manage their investments. Accredited investors should be able to withstand a total loss of their high risk investment. They should know when and where to get professional help.

Merely receiving a designation of accredited investor can expose an unsophisticated investor to danger. For example, many enticing AIs have a minimum investment of $500,000 or even just $250,000. If you barely meet the minimum with $1,000,000 of net worth and then put 50%, or even 25%, of your entire wealth into one high risk investment, you would be extremely overconcentrated in that one investment. If you were to put a more reasonable percentage into an AI, for example 5%, then you really ought to have over $5,000,000 before considering an AI at $250,000.

Be aware that if you are an accredited investor, sales representatives will find you. You may get solicitations in the mail for investment presentations which you must be accredited to attend. A financial advisor may introduce you to the sales representative for a new investment opportunity only for accredited investors. Again, consult your most trusted advisors.

Hedge fund

A *hedge fund* is the general term for the diverse funds that sell to accredited investors and institutions. Many hedge funds are run by famous managers who came from mutual funds. These managers jump to hedge funds for the higher income they can make and the freedom to use riskier investment techniques not allowed at mutual funds. Other hedge fund managers developed a following from their stock newsletters or blogs, which allowed them to find investors. There are thousands of hedge funds; it is relatively easy for entrepreneurial people to start a hedge fund.

Hedge funds often have a short-term, quick-return investing strategy. Despite this, your money could be locked up for a year or more and only available during redemption periods. In pursuit of high returns and to earn their high fees, hedge funds managers use aggressive, risky strategies. They often highly concentrate their investments in their best ideas, which could be only a few stocks. Their tools include derivatives, options, and debt leverage. Hedge fund strategies fall along the following lines:

- Long-short equity strategy: A hedge fund owns stock A in a *long* position. The fund can also sell stock B that it does not own, setting up a *short* position. The fund borrows stock B (thereby incurring a debt), sells it, and later must buy it back to return the borrowed stock; all with the expectation that the price will drop. (Mutual funds can not take short positions.) Combining long and short positions can allow the fund potentially to generate profit in volatile markets and down markets.

- Activist: The hedge fund accumulates a large long stock position in an undervalued or distressed company, perhaps 2% to 10% of the outstanding stock, giving it influence over management. The activist fund manager tries to make changes at the company to raise the stock price. The fund may force cost cutting and layoffs, key management changes, or a capital restructuring such as paying out horded cash or taking on more debt. The fund may force the company to spin off underperforming divisions or to sell itself to another company.

- Arbitrage: Arbitragers exploit price misalignments in the market. (We described ETF arbitrage previously in the discussion on trading ETFs.) As an example, suppose the U.S. dollar rises 0.20%

against the Euro, the U.S. dollar rises 0.19% against the British pound, and meanwhile the Euro and British pound exchange rate remains unchanged. Then a fund could use dollars to buy Euros, use those Euros to buy pounds, and then use the pounds to buy back more dollars than it started with. Such arbitrage exchanges will drive the exchange rates to realign.

- Emerging markets: These hedge funds look for mispriced stocks in volatile emerging markets. One strategy is to find growing stocks flying under the radar of analysts, which allows greater mispricing of local stocks. The hope is the company grows and attracts wider attention resulting in its stock price rising. The risk here is that these stocks fail to grow or that the foreign market or government is unstable.

- Managed futures: The futures contract is an agreement upon a price for a future delivery of a commodity. A grower, who wants an assured profit on his wheat crop, can strike a contract with a miller, who wants to stabilize his future costs for wheat—both gain an economic benefit. Hedge funds buy and sell futures contracts to bet on price movements of the underlying commodity. They have no intention of delivering or receiving the wheat, so they have to close out their contract positions before the delivery date, regardless of the price, taking a gain or loss.

- Momentum: These hedge funds couple momentum investing with computer prowess. They use computers to spot a nascent price trend before other funds and race to place orders to ride the trend. To profit, they devise algorithms to spot buying and selling behaviors of institutions, other hedge funds, and even the collective action of individual traders. They must get their order in before other players and before the trend dissipates. They use the fastest computers and networks available. They will even try to situate their computers as close to the computers of the exchanges as possible for a millisecond advantage in the race to place orders.

- Fund of funds: These funds invest in other hedge funds. A fund of funds offers a diversification across hedge fund strategies that you by yourself might not be able to achieve due to the minimum investment required at each hedge fund. The fund of funds adds its own high fee on top of the high fees at the individual hedge funds that the fund of funds buys. In my opinion, the addition of a second layer of fees is too high a hurdle, and you should pass on this strategy.

Hedge funds are all about their managers. Your investment in a hedge fund is primarily a bet on the acumen of the fund's managers, that they can out-trade their counterparts at other hedge funds or at mutual funds. Their tactical buying and selling treats investing like winning a chess game, and it is the opposite of investing in an economic engine of a company that builds value. (We will discuss economic engines in a later chapter on equity strategies.)

Private equity
Private equity funds generally invest in private companies not listed on the public stock exchanges. Private equity funds make highly concentrated, sometimes one-of-a-kind investments. To control the inherent risk, they rely on their ability to evaluate a company and to fix its problems with better management or added resources.

One private equity fund strategy could be described as "corporate engineering." They will buy an entire company or a division of a large company. They will acquire and merge two companies to grow them faster than either could independently. They will try to rehabilitate troubled companies. They will buy a public company and take it private in a leveraged buyout (LBO). In a LBO, the fund will buy all the stock of a company, often using debt leverage, cancel the stock, and delist it from the exchanges. The company can then execute an improvement strategy relieved of the need for quarterly earnings performance to please stockholders.

In another strategy, private equity funds develop commercial real estate. These funds build or buy and remodel shopping centers, retirement homes, student housing, or office buildings. They renovate luxury hotels in Europe. They can create companies to build infrastructure like access roads, warehouses, or shipping docks in a developing country.

Private equity strategies require time to execute. These private equity funds require a lockup period of seven or more years. So, your return will be at the back-end after the maturation of the strategy.

Venture capital

Investing in *venture capital* (VC) funds is not available to the average accredited investor. VC funds generally raise their money from financial institutions, pension funds, and ultrawealthy individuals. VC funds invest in start-up companies, the riskiest of all companies, most of which fail. Also, ultrawealthy individuals sometimes invest independently as *angel investors*, who are the earliest investors in a start-up at the conception stage. Angel investors contribute their knowledge as well as their money.

Alternative investment fees

Alternative investment fees are very high. They are a drain on the potential return from your investment that only the highest performance can overcome. The fees vary widely based on the type of AI, the renown of the manager, the reputation of the management firm, and the performance history.

AI fees usually have three parts. First, there is the sales commission for the sales representative and the financial advisor. This can range from 1% to 5% of the invested amount. Then, the ongoing fee of the AI fund basically includes a management fee of 2% of assets and a performance fee of 20% of any gain. Some funds charge more than 2% and 20%. The management fee is always paid, while the performance fee is paid only if there is a gain. Some funds feature a *high-water mark*, where any loss has to be made up before the performance fee can be charged. However, with so many hedge funds competing for investors, the trend has been for AI fees to come down, especially for new hedge funds.

The performance fee paid only on a gain is not as desirable for the investor as it first appears. With a 20% incentive for gains and no penalty for losses, a hedge fund manager is motivated to take great risks with little to lose. The manager gets a huge fee on any gain, while the investor takes all the losses, and the manager is still paid her 2% management fee regardless. The interests of the investor and the manager are not properly aligned. A better arrangement for the investor would be a flat fee of 1% or 2% of the assets being managed. Then if the investor's portfolio gains 15%, the manager gains 15% on her fee, and if the investor loses 9%, then the manager's fee goes down 9%. Now the interests of investor and manager are aligned.

Also, a high-water mark intended to protect the investor can backfire. Say, a top hedge fund manager suffers a large loss during an economic recession or from very risky investments gone bad, it could take him years to recoup the loss. Rather than wait years for his performance fee to come back, a highly sought after manager can quit the fund and join another hedge fund making a fresh start. You, meanwhile, have lost a talented manager.

AI fees vary from one fund to another, are complicated, and only add to the difficulty of evaluating an AI investment. AI's are the province of very wealthy, sophisticated investors.

Part Four

Getting started investing

In the previous chapters, you learned how to assess yourself as an investor and to set clear goals for yourself. You further learned about the critical value of time, counting real assets versus imaginary value, and the basics of risk, Now you are ready to begin investing. In the following chapters we will help you find, research, and evaluate specific investment assets. We will then show you how to build up a robust portfolio that mitigates risks.

As we proceed, you will discover missing skills you need to acquire. You may already have some idea of skills you lack based on your self-assessment. However, be reassured that if you have understood what you have read thus far in this book, you can learn to do basic investment research. You should approach investment research pretty much as you did in school preparing to write a research paper. The more stocks, ETFs, bonds, and mutual funds you research the better you will become. If you decide you want help, we will discuss where to get professional help.

The first asset decisions people typically face center on mutual funds and stocks. When they begin a new job, they must choose the mutual funds for their 401k plan, which for most people has been an exercise in guessing. When they start their IRA (individual retirement account) they usually look for stocks, mutual funds, and ETFs.

We will get started investing by looking for reliable sources of information for your investigations. Then we will explore how to select individual investment assets beginning with stocks and expanding from there.

Find reliable information sources

One of the main advantages that professional investors have over the rest of us is they have more and better information on potential investments. Your skill in gathering information will be the foundation of your investing success. You must be resourceful, even creative, in gathering information. You must vet your information sources and be very careful what and whom you depend on. In particular, you need to judge the motivations of the information source, what pressures might they be facing. You must always maintain a healthy skepticism while evaluating their information. Be especially wary of what you see in the media. Review the earlier discussion of who do you trust.

Reports to and from government

For ascertaining long term trends, you will discover that the most reliable information comes from U.S. government agencies. These include the Federal Reserve (FED), U.S. Census Bureau, Bureau of Economic Analysis, Bureau of Labor Statistics, and many others. You can visit their websites for a wealth of information, including interest rates, employment figures, economic data, and historical trends. Every serious analyst uses and relies on government data. The agencies have the professional staff and resources to gather and verify the data in their reports, and they apply well established methodologies. The main disadvantage is that it takes time to verify and analyze the volume of data. The trade-off is accuracy versus timeliness. So, they will issue initial quick reports and issue revised reports as needed. Though the bureaus can be pressured by congressional or executive political meddling, the reports tend to be professionally methodical. Similarly, the governments of major countries and the United Nations provide the best data in those regions.

In evaluating a stock or a mutual fund, the most important and reliable information comes in the financial statements required by government agencies, such as the SEC, from businesses such as banks, manufacturers, service companies, and retail companies. The financial statement is a part of a company's annual report. The financial statement includes the balance sheet, income statement, cash flow, earnings, and detailed explanatory notes. The financial statement is audited by an outside accounting firm which provides an independent opinion on the statement's reliability. In the annual report, the financial statement is supplemented by management's discussion of that financial data and of company strategy and products. If you seriously plan to analyze stocks yourself, you will need to take some finance classes to learn to read financial statements. When you become knowledgeable, you can also look at a company's 10-K report for even greater financial detail. The annual report is available on the company or mutual fund website.

Commercial information sources and academia

After the reports from the government or required by the government, the next tier of information comes from sources like industrial and professional associations, investment rating companies, research and advisory companies, and academia.

The websites of *industrial and professional associations* are great sources of industry background and history. Evaluating a stock means researching the company and the industry it competes in. These websites have information on industry trends, new products, hot issues, and competition between companies. You can get a good idea of who the leaders are and who the innovators and disruptors are. Do recognize, however, that associations are often advocates for their industries, so you must consider the politics behind the information. You can find these websites by doing a search for industrial associations, professional associations, or manufacturer associations. You can be more specific and search for publishing, food service, or plumbing company associations, or for labor union websites. From there you can obtain subscriptions to industry journals and newsletters.

The *investment rating company* sells proprietary reports to its clients. Two examples of rating companies are Standard and Poor's and Moody's, which are famous for their bond ratings that we discussed previously. They and other such firms, like Value Line and Morningstar, sell financial analysis and ratings on companies, their stocks and bonds, and on mutual funds. They strive for impartial, dependable ratings. They also produce estimates of future revenues, earnings, and target prices. I recommend that you treat their financial analyses and their ratings as informed, reasonable estimates, and not as the final word. As you become familiar with each of them, you will begin to see their particular subtle biases, which you can account for in your own evaluations. You can subscribe to these services yourself, or you might find their reports at your public library reference desk.

Another commercial source of information is the *research and advisory company*. Respected companies include Gartner, McKinsey & Company, and boutique firms like The Linley Group. These research and advisory companies sell subscription reports and topical studies about the products and business strategies of the companies that they cover. The research and advisory company will consult with clients to refine product ideas and competitive strategy. Their reports typically focus on a firm's products and business rather than its stocks or bonds. Their reports provide an independent assessment of the industries that they cover, and their research and opinions are often quoted in news articles in the media. These are expensive services for an individual subscription, though you may have access to their reports through the company where you work. The research and advisory companies will also produce specially commissioned reports for their clients. However, any specially commissioned report that you are likely to see will tend to favor the commissioning client, as an unfavorable report will not be distributed by that client. There are many commercial research and advisory companies, and they vary widely in quality depending on the expertise of their analysts. I recommend that you study any such company by reading reviews of that company and reading several of its reports to form your own opinion of their expertise and reliability before investing based on their information.

You will occasionally see investment advice based on *university research studies*. These can be economic studies by professors or even by graduate students. You must read these studies with skepticism, as academics often pursue their own theory to the rejection of other lines of thinking. The quality of the research can also vary widely with the experience of the researcher. You will likely encounter academic papers second hand as they are reported in the media or quoted by a company. These second hand accounts are prone to misinterpretation and spin by the media or the marketing staff who quote them. This is in part because academic research papers are written for other academics who are already knowledgeable of the context of the research. Lacking this background perspective, media and marketing staff can misinterpret the import of the academic study. Before you commit your money, you may want to find and read the original academic study for yourself. You may discover that the report itself may contradict the given advice supposedly based on that report.

Research from investment firms

Investment firms include mutual funds, hedge funds, insurance companies, and any company that invests a pool of money, such as Berkshire Hathaway. Investment firms buy stocks and bonds, so their analysts are tasked to find investments that are most likely to increase in value. Often referred to as *buy-side* analysts, their job is close to what you must do as an individual investor—pick good stocks or bonds and avoid undue risk and mistakes. When you read or see an interview with any analyst, you must determine if she is a buy-side or a sell-side analyst (to be discussed in the next section), as their responsibilities are very different. Generally, your needs as an individual investor align more closely with the stock recommendations from buy-side analysts, who must pick winners to buy. Use their stock recommendations as a starting idea for your own research and evaluation.

However, care is required. Buy-side analysts generally do not publish reports for public consumption. You will learn of their ideas mostly from media reports. By the time you hear about their stock picks, the investment firm will already have made their buys. There is no advantage for the firm to release their prospective buys in advance, when competitors, like you, can buy the stock and drive up the price. Likewise, you will seldom hear about it when they sell a stock until afterward. For you, their most useful recommendations will be for stocks they believe have long-term potential, that they anticipate continuing to buy and accumulate over time.

Research from brokerages

Brokerage firms like Morgan Stanley, Goldman Sachs, UBS, and Merrill Lynch are known for providing full service to their clients. These national brokerages are sometimes referred to as a "wirehouse," an old term which predates modern computer networks. Their financial advisors provide services ranging from recommending stocks for a client's consideration to completely taking over and running a client's account. Their financial advisors are supported by research staff who publish detailed reports with individual stock and bond recommendations, as well as recommendations for the whole range of investment assets. The investment analysts at brokerages are often referred to *sell-side* analysts. Their recommendations are eagerly picked up and reported by the media, and the brokerages promote the reputation of their research staff.

However, individual investors like you and me are only one type of client at a large brokerage. Hedge funds and mutual funds can conduct their trades through the big brokerages as their *prime broker*, so the buy-side analyst can also be a client of the sell-side analyst. A brokerage with an *investment bank* division will also have corporate clients. The sell-side analyst has the added responsibility of helping attract clients to the prime brokerage and the investment bank. The sell-side analyst will provide stock recommendations to individual clients as well as to buy-side analysts, who use the reports as one source of ideas. A respected sell-side analyst covering an industry helps the investment bank win clients from that industry. The sell-side analyst needs to maintain a long-term working relationship with the companies that he is assigned to cover. He also does not want to offend a client of the investment bank, so he wants to avoid issuing a negative report that upsets the company.

What this means for you in interpreting reports from brokerages is that they tend to rate stocks on inoffensive scales, such as "most preferred" to "least preferred" or "timely" to "untimely". You will seldom see an outright "sell" recommendation, though the lowest rating on their scale may mean just that. When the media reports a change in a brokerage analyst's stock rating, it will often lead to a strong movement in the stock's price. As a practical matter, a change in the sell-side analyst's rating is more immediately consequential than the actual rating, often resulting in a large price movement that same day. You might want to talk with a financial advisor at the brokerage issuing the recommendation to see if the stock is suitable for your portfolio; the financial advisor may offer further insight into the analyst's thinking, from direct conversation with the analyst.

Media information sources

L et me say at the outset that you should exercise great caution with what you hear and see in the media. Media sources are where most nonprofessional investors get most of their information. The investing world is overflowing with media trying to tell you how to invest—from the Wall Street Journal, to cable television, to internet bloggers, to investing magazines and newsletters, to this book. The internet has only made the situation worse by allowing absolutely anyone to set up an investing blog. Rather than make a list of who is reliable and who is not, I will introduce several methods to help you sort through it. You need to determine for yourself which sources you find reliable, because ultimately it is your money at risk.

Credentials

You should look at the credentials of any writer or any person being interviewed. In the noisy world of investments, the following specific licenses and certifications are most relevant to the individual investor and are earned through course work and examination:

- CFA—Chartered Financial Analyst (for investment management)
- CFP—Certified Financial Planner (for personal financial planning)
- Series 7, and Series 63, Series 65, etc. licenses (registration to conduct security transactions)
- CPA—Certified Public Accountant (licensed by state board of accountancy)
- EA—Enrolled Agent (IRS credential to represent taxpayers)

The above licenses and certifications are respected credentials either in investing or in taxation, so you know the author or speaker has a foundation of training and knowledge. Note that a CPA or EA is tax trained, but they are not investment advisors. Conversely, a CFA, CFP, or Series 7 and Series 6x licensed financial advisor is investment trained, but they are not tax advisors. Also, you might consider writers or speakers with:

- CIMA—Certified Investment Management Analyst (focus on management analytics)
- MBA—Master of Business Administration degree (from a major university)
- Government agency spokesperson
- Title and years of relevant investment experience at a major investment firm

Upon finding these credentials, you can then proceed to evaluate what the writer or speaker says on its merits.

You will also encounter an alphabet soup of other similar sounding honorifics given by many organizations. These you will need to research and carefully screen for yourself. Note that a "PhD" or "Doctor" or "lawyer" may be in a field unrelated to investing. Previous publication of articles, newsletters, and books is of limited help in assessing an author's credentials or reliability. Testimonials can be solicited and screened. Sponsored seminars (regardless of who the sponsor is) often are disguised sales events.

Investing books

Hundreds of investing books have been written. A few are acknowledged classics. When I first started investing, I read a classic investing book and followed its advice—and lost my money. My point is that there is no replacing learning from experience. By all means, read a variety of classic investing books, learn all you can. However, some books espouse theories and complicated techniques that you are not ready for, but maybe in a decade you might be. Other books promote investing systems that upon careful scrutiny are based on chance. Other books promote investment systems that are not appropriate for you, because they are short-term and high-risk trading schemes. Avoid get-rich-quick books. Ignore books that turn out to be a sales pitch for an investing service that they want you to buy.

I recommend you start by reading (college textbooks) about basic finance and economics (start with macroeconomics as opposed to microeconomics). It may seem like a slow, unexciting start, but the more you learn, the better you will be able to sort out the nonsense books.

Seminars and lectures

Many investment seminars and lectures are educational and even entertaining. You have the best chance of seminars being educationally motivated, when they are offered by a college as a class for unit credit. Many investment lectures and seminars (regardless of who the sponsor is) are advertised as educational, but the intent is to secure a sales appointment with you. Approach any seminar, read any invitation, with a sense of "What are they selling?" or even "Can this be for real?" In a live presentation, a great salesman can overwhelm people in the audience and make sales that you never would otherwise have considered. As with all media, skip seminars and lectures that claim they will show you how to get rich.

Magazines, newsletters, internet blogs, TV, and radio

When you see a media article, you should note the role of the author. You should determine if the writer is reporting news, interviewing someone, or giving his own opinion. Is she objectively reporting news events, facts, or economic statistics? Is he reporting news and then adding commentary? Is he acting as an interviewer or is he engaging in a discussion with the guest? Is she a pundit who is offering her own opinion? Separate the writer's opinion from fact, and separate the interviewer's opinion from the opinion of the interviewee. Check the credentials of both the writer and the interviewee. For internet articles, click on the author's name to read her bio, and do a web search on the interviewee. Always remember that most of the media articles you see will be written by reporters who were likely journalism majors.

As you peruse the media, I suggest you pay particular attention to interviews of buy-side analysts and mutual fund portfolio managers for the reasons discussed previously.

The "media" includes newspapers, stock newsletters, websites, and magazines. It includes broadcast and cable TV, the internet, and radio. It includes purveyors of stock picks and advocates of any stock picking system, whether graphical or quantitative. It includes all pundits and commenting personalities.

Caveat emptor! The right of free speech means there may be no editorial oversight or quality control of what is being said in mass media in print or on the internet, to wit:

- Literally, anyone can start an investing newsletter in print or blog on the internet.
- Anyone can pick stocks and promote a list of alleged winning stocks.
- Many investment websites on the internet let hobbyists and students post articles.
- Anyone can claim a self-given title like CEO of their own investing business.
- Regarding publicized stock picks, there's no telling how much resource and insight went into that analysis.
- Search engines provide no guidance on the quality of the investing articles that they list.

White noise, information, insight

As you research a company or any other investment, one of the hardest skills that takes the most time to learn is recognizing meaningful information in the flood of data. As we mean it here, data is the massive collection of facts, statistics, and news, while information is that key data from which you can make a decision. There is a tremendous volume of economic data dispensed every week, every day. Most of it is white noise and useless. Discerning information is a key skill in the art of investing.

Similarly, finding an insight to guide an investment decision is rare among the banter of stock analysts and pundits. I suggest that you treat the stock analysis and recommendations by media stock commentators as you would sports analysis and predictions by former star athletes and coaches who are now media sports commentators. Much of the commentary will be repetitive and superficial. Their predictions, whether for stocks or ball games, are just as likely to pan out.

In the following discussion, I will give you some perspective to help you discern information from data, and some tells to spot potentially weak analysis and commentary.

Press cycle burden results in distortions

The media operates under the press deadline. With each press cycle they have to fill their blank pages and empty air time with fresh content. One result is the constant reporting of the movement of the S&P 500, the Dow Jones, and other indices. This overreporting of market statistics imparts a seeming importance to them, when in fact these too frequent reports are mostly white noise. News anchors constantly ask their interview guests for the reasons for today's market movements, and the guest will oblige with comments about the market reacting to the day's news event, whatever it may be. Yet, there may be no causal relationship, just more white noise linking some convenient news item to some random index movement. So, unless an index moves more than, say, 3% in a day or 10% in a week, the constant ups and downs are not really noteworthy; they're no more than bumps in the road.

Reporting versus prediction

A typical media business report offers the day's economic statistics and events. Then a commentator will explain what he thinks it means for the market going forward. The analyst prediction is a popular media trope. Investors are so fearful of the unknown future, they wish for fortune tellers. However, on any given day, you will hear one commentator predicting the market goes up, while another commentator predicts it going down. Sometimes, two dueling analysts will be featured on the same program. It makes for lively entertainment with little useful information, though their contrasting explanations of the dynamics of the market could be instructive.

For all intents and purposes, no one can predict where the market will go. You need to sort out data and event reporting from commentator analysis, opinion, and prediction.

Tells of analysts and pundits

Media investment commentators try to offer insights into the market. Their analysis can be sound and helpful to you in understanding what is happening in the market and economy. At the least, it should make sense to you at the level of understanding you have currently attained. Other times the commentary is weak. Look for the following tells that an analyst or pundit might be overcompensating for a weak idea or is wrong.

- A forceful and even strident presentation can convey the appearance of authority and knowledge. It may convince some listeners that the analyst or pundit knows better and may deter challenges from the audience. Just as likely, it may conceal gaps or limits in the knowledge of the speaker.

- Use of jargon to imply a higher expertise. For example, an analyst's use of "constructive" which just means "like," as in "I am constructive on that stock" instead of simply "I like that stock." Applying a marketing name like "smart beta" to a fund strategy. (A classic example in telecom is the term POTS for "plain old telephone service.")
- Overemphasizing how important their commentary is. Repeatedly saying "Now this is important ..."
- They don't understand the concept. The substitution of "volatility" for personal investment risk. The misuse of "beta" to imply a growth stock. Or, the misuse of "inflection point" to mean a market bottom or top instead of a turning point (an inflection point can not be at the top or bottom of a curve).
- The incorrect use of statistics or charts. For example, the use of insignificant data (low R-squared), or the misuse of a wind rose chart in place of a bar chart or line chart.

You may spot other tells that alert you to be cautious of a pundit's commentary.

Salesmen's tricks

Great salesmen show great conviction in their product. If you perceive they sincerely believe it, then you are more likely to believe it too. They will repeat their conviction, because if you hear it often enough, you may come to accept it.

Some salesmen will tell you what you want to hear, what you want to believe. They will tell you they have an easy, surefire product leading to investing riches.

Media analysts and pundits know these tricks. They will show conviction in their opinions and predictions. You need to reason out for yourself whether what they are so convinced of is really applicable to you. Their conviction is an emotional layer for you to cut away in order to evaluate the merit of what they are saying.

Sellers of stock picking products know these tricks. They boast their stock method and track record. This includes many purveyors of famous websites, investment newspapers and newsletters, stock picking software, and how-to-trade-stock classes. They all express supreme confidence that you will make money easily by subscribing to their website, buying their investing software, or paying for their class. They build up their reputations through advertising. Just remember that the best stock investors are turning away clients, they don't need to advertise and self-promote.

Hapdiction and prediction

Stock picking newsletters and other paid-for services will advertise a special "system" for picking stock winners. You should take such claims with extreme skepticism. One way to construct a "winning record" is simply to make a lot of predictions and highlight just the ones that randomly worked out. Such aleatory results are not credible predictions but random outcomes that coincided with the prognostication. We shall coin a new word here and call such an outcome a *hapdiction*, meaning a prediction that happens to come true by pure unrelated chance. An example of hapdiction is where stocks picked by throwing darts at a stock list beat the market. One famous example of hapdiction is the Super Bowl indicator, where the winner of the Super Bowl has successfully hapdicted an up or down year for the market with 80% accuracy. An actionable prediction should be more scientific and based on study, observation, and experience that identifies an economic cause and effect.

Yet, because at any given time any given stock or the entire market has basically a 50%-50% chance of going up or down, hapdictions can appear no less accurate than predictions based on research and knowledge. Long-running correlations like the Super Bowl indicator appear to lend credence even to nonsensical hapdiction systems. Several well-known stock selection systems are more or less hapdictive in nature. We will briefly discuss them before we move on to fundamental stock analysis.

Momentum investing
Momentum investing is the idea of identifying a stock price trend and trading based on the expected continuation of that trend. The key is to find an up trend, buy before the trend is widely recognized, and sell when it

reverses (or the opposite for a down trend). Spotting a trend at its earliest and speed of order execution are critical to success in momentum investing. Traders using the fastest computer algorithms and computer networks have a substantial advantage. Momentum investing is a staple of hedge funds (see the previous discuss of hedge fund momentum trading). Many subscription services and news dailies also try to identify trending stocks, but on a different timescale compared to hedge funds. Momentum trends are relatively short-lived and begin and end unpredictably. This describes an inherently chaotic process. Momentum traders look for trends when they happen, rather than predict trends. Riding a trend assumption is basically a hapdiction technique.

Technical analysis and charting

Technical analysis is based on a stock's price movements along with the volume of shares traded. The technician does not look into the company, its management, its products, nor its financial reports. The technician looks only at stock price movements and volume searching for known patterns that herald an up or down movement in the stock price. The prime assumption of technical analysis is that the stock price and volume reflect everything that affects the stock; in other words, the market price of the stock accounts for all influencing factors including the stock's fundamentals, the general economic climate, and the psychology of buyers and sellers. This assumption is a version of the efficient market hypothesis. The second assumption is that price movements follow trends with patterns that repeat themselves. Trading is based on the expected repetition of the price movement pattern.

Charting is an implementation of technical analysis done graphically on stock charts of price movements and trading volume. Chartists look for stock price patterns such as "head and shoulders," "triangle," "double tops," "double bottoms," or "cup and handle," and many others that signal a possible stock price move. These charts are widely available through the internet and subscription charting services. When you see stock price charts with technical lines drawn above or below the price curve or forming a triangle, those typically relate to searching for chart patterns. The overlay of Fibonacci retracement lines to find resistance or support levels is a chartist technique. Chartists also use curve smoothing techniques such as hundred-day moving averages, boundary lines, or X-O charts in order to exposed patterns obscured by the noise of daily stock movements.

Both of the key assumptions of technical analysis have been subject to criticism and debate. The efficient market hypothesis is controversial. It depends on the thorough and timely distribution of all information to all buyers and sellers. For instance, do you believe you are equally as well informed and knowledgeable as any mutual fund manager, anyone in government, anyone at work, or any neighbor? Do you or they have the computer software to conduct technical analysis? I, for one, believe market inefficiencies do exist that successful investment managers do exploit.

The case for the efficacy of technical and chart patterns is largely anecdotal. I have found too few academic studies of technical analysis to draw any conclusions. However, in addition to the questions about the key assumptions, I have several concerns about technical analysis and charting:

- In many charting examples, the finding of a pattern or of support or resistance levels seems to be in the eye of the beholder. This makes it very much a subjective judgment.
- When a chart pattern is recognized, the decision to trade is still left up to the your own instincts, which allows other influences to affect your decision. (Not necessarily a bad thing, since you should consider all other factors.)
- The technical information in a stock price line is obscured by daily trading noise, so smoothing techniques like moving averages or X-O charts are applied. These smoothing techniques remove data detail and, hence, reduce information content. These are rudimentary techniques compared to the advanced statistical data analysis and curve fitting methods used by hedge funds.
- Technical analysis focuses on the shape of data to find patterns. This becomes a study of metadata (data about data, pictures of

data) rather than study of what underlies the data to cause the stock price to move.

- Looking solely at the stock price movement and volume seems insufficient. That is analogous to trying to predict the weather looking just at the temperature and air pressure—not even looking out the window. Only with the advancement of satellite weather photos did weather forecasting accuracy leap forward. One should look at all the other relevant economic variables, such as earnings reports, company announcements, government actions, and interest rates to get a greater picture.

For these concerns as well as lacking an economic cause-and-effect narrative to anticipate price movements, technical analysis and charting are hapdictive techniques for stock selection.

Part Five

How to pick and buy your own stocks

Once you know how to find reliable sources of information, you are ready to identify candidate investments for your investigation. We will start with company stocks.

Get ready to do some work. You will need to pick a trial company to practice on as you read through these steps. You will need to dig as deeply as it takes for you to make a decision you can have confidence in and live with, without anxiety.

Finding stock ideas

From the previous chapters you should begin to see plenty of sources for stock ideas for your research candidates (as well as companies to avoid). Start here:

- Mutual funds: Find actively managed mutual funds and look at their stock holdings, with particular attention to the larger holdings by dollar amount. From the annual reports read the portfolio managers' commentary on their holdings. They have researched and chosen these stocks. Which companies are bought by multiple funds? For this purpose, do not go to index mutual funds or ETFs, as those stocks were bought solely because they were listed in an index without regard to the company's performance. Note that I am not suggesting that you imitate the investments of any mutual fund manager, only use the holdings list as a source of ideas for your own research. By the time you see a report of a mutual fund's holdings, the manager may well have already sold any of the stocks on that dated list.
- Industry journals and websites: Who are the industry leaders, innovators, and disruptors? Which company's management is respected, which criticized? Who is introducing a revolutionary new product? Which companies are the old guard; are they thriving, just surviving, or dying? What product piques your interest or even gets you excited?
- Brokerage recommendations: Each brokerage publishes lists of recommended stocks. They will have a recommended list of dividend-paying companies, a list of growth companies, and other focused lists. What is their rationale for each company? How long

do companies stay recommended on that list, how stable is that list, do companies come and go? Stock ideas may come from your financial advisor as well; are they from his own research, or does he use the brokerage recommended stocks?

- Research and advisory company reports: Which companies do they praise, which do they criticize? Are leading companies identified? Have they identified a new trend in an industry?

- Your personal experience with a company: Were you impressed with a company's product or service (whether at work or at home)? Did you have an outstanding experience with them? Was this unique to you or available to all their customers? How do they stack up against their competitors? Would you buy from them again?

- Look at what has and is happening all around you: A new type of car is coming (like the minivan, electric car, driverless car); all the kids are abuzz about the newest gadget (iPod) or movie (*Frozen*); a revolutionary faucet with just one handle; the shift of retailing to the internet; genetically modified foods; 3-d printing in manufacturing; water shortages and water purification; containerized shipping; arthroscopic surgery; and so forth. Look for new investment possibilities everywhere. What company will exploit the new thing?

Be patient. Don't worry that investable ideas are few and far between, just be open and alert to see one when it comes.

You will often find conflicting opinions about the same company. Don't be discouraged or flustered if you do encounter different judgments. Just study their rationale and use it as the starting point for your own research and evaluation.

The media is an endless river of stock picks. See the previous discussion of media information services. While some analyst interview might provide an interesting long-term stock idea, for the most part you should be very selective about recommendations you find in media sources. Media articles tend to focus on popular, even trendy stocks. They often focus on short-term trading of stocks or options and discuss hapdictive chart signals. Many stock articles are written by amateurs, while other articles are computer generated, plugging a company's vital statistics into a preformatted article with preformatted tables; both little more than lorem ipsum.

Treat recommendations from relatives and friends as if the idea were from media sources. Discuss the stock with them and then go do your own research to determine for yourself whether it can move you toward your goals.

Screening tools

The quick screen can eliminate a lot of redundant work. Professional investors will use computer programs to screen hundreds of companies looking for those few that match preset criteria. If you research a lot of companies, you may want to tailor a personal version of the quick screen with the stock screening tools available on the internet. However, rather than using the screen to find a desultory list of candidate companies, I suggest using the screening tool to eliminate weak companies that come to your attention from your research sources. While you may not at this stage be ready to determine your quick screen criteria, you will by the end of this book have a better idea how to begin to do so. You will be refining your screening criteria over time, particularly as you study company financial reports and as your needs change.

You will find that some screening tools are better suited to your criteria. Some tools are better for fundamental analysis, while other tools are oriented toward technical analysis.

Evaluating a company

The evaluation method we will outline here is called *fundamental analysis*, where we look at a company's business essentials. This is the company analysis taught in graduate business schools. For our example, we will use *The Walt Disney Company* (Disney), a company most readers will already be somewhat familiar with. The fundamental analysis process will be the same for any other candidate company.

I recommend as we proceed that you first pick an interesting trial company from your information sources. For your first stock, I suggest you start with a dividend-paying company. As we go through the research and evaluation process with Disney, you can practice on your trial company applying the methods we discuss. You can compare the two companies, just as you would in deciding between any two companies to invest in.

Note that evaluating a company is not a one time exercise. You will regularly need to check up on every company that you own at least once a year, when the annual report is issued. Each time you reevaluate, you will decide anew if you still want to own this company. Note also that evaluating a company is a learned skill and that your skill will improve with practice, just like playing the piano.

Does the company fit you

You want to invest in companies that you can root for. Sometimes a company just doesn't fit your world view. Will you be happy owning your trial company? Examples of companies that some people object to are tobacco companies, munitions companies, polluting companies, alcoholic beverage companies, gambling companies, and unhealthy-food companies. Often these shunned companies offer a higher dividend yield, because their unpopularity results in a lower stock price. Financial advisors will recommended them for their boosted yield, and for some income investors these companies represent an opportunity to reap aberrantly higher dividends. You will want to decide if you can "support" these companies and act accordingly. If you can not support a company, then that investment decision becomes a personal choice.

On the other hand, you may like a company because it aligns with your social or political views. You should resist the temptation to overvalue a company based on social or political activism. Examples might be companies that build low-income housing, produce renewable energy, run charter schools, or recycle waste. By all means, add these companies to your candidate list. Then, evaluate every candidate company solely on its businesses merits.

Generally, Disney is a very popular company, with few who object to it. Yet, there will be protestors against some aspect of its policies, as a web search will readily show. In evaluating Disney, we look to see if these protests can disrupt its business or do long-term harm to its reputation. At the time of this writing, Disney does not appear threatened by such activity.

Products and services

In evaluating your trial company you should be able to state clearly what the product is that the company truly sells and what their customer is buying. This is not as trivial as it sounds, because often the value is not just in the physical good or the service delivered. Gucci stores, Budweiser beer, and Glamour magazine all sell a self-image along with the handbag, the beer, or the magazine. A travel company might sell adventure, culture, safety, or convenience. Understanding what the company really sells can help you spot an intangible product problem even as the physical good or service remains the same.

Discovering the true product or service that a company sells is the key to evaluating a company's potential growth. Amazon on its website sells the same products online that are available in retail stores or even on other websites. Try to clearly state what is the true product or service that prompts you or other customers to return to Amazon.

Disney sells movies, broadcast TV, cable TV, sports channels, and vacations to its theme parks and resorts. Disney also sells, and the customer buys, intangibles such as happy vacation memories and families bonding together.

Let's look at the product considerations for Disney, as well as for your trial company:

- How well does your trial company draw repeat buyers of its products or services to support its revenues and cash flow? Disney certainly does rely on repeat customers. Its movie franchises, like *Star Wars*, draw fans to multiple movie sequels and spinoffs from the main story arc. Its animation classics draw a new generation of young viewers every four or five years, and it has remade cartoon classics into live action movies. Its ESPN sports service relies on the repeat viewing habits of sports fans. The theme parks have a critical repeat-customer base among the local population in addition to the once-in-a-lifetime out-of-state vacationers.

  Pharmaceutical companies love drugs that need to be taken for life, such as cholesterol lowering drugs or blood pressure drugs. On the other hand, vaccines are given once, and antibiotics are taken only as needed for the occasional infection. Sports manufacturers come out with new models of tennis racquets every few years in order to encourage players to upgrade to newer racquets. What is the likely success of the new products?

  What is the rationale for continued customer demand? Is the product a necessity like food, clothing, or fuel? Does the product rely on a fad that can vanish with a change in fashion? Is the product a value-added industrial component like ball bearings, passenger seats, or jet engines? Is it a commodity like lumber, rubber, copper, and oil? Will the service be needed into the future like janitorial services, dentistry, food delivery, or travel agents?

- How strong is your company's next product cycle? Intel steadily introduces next generation computer microprocessors on a well-publicized calendar. Apple introduced a series of category-changing products with the iPod, iTunes, and iPhone. Delays in introducing new cell phones allowed Motorola's competitors to take away its customers with flashier products. Kodak and Fuji film lost out to digital cameras. Swiss watch makers ignored the new digital watches. Boeing takes up to a decade to introduce a next generation passenger airliner; its product cycle is completely visible as progress or delays on a new airplane are widely reported. How is your company sustaining its product line into the future?

Disney plans out a steady stream of replacement products to refresh its product line. Disney constantly makes new films, creates new characters, typically with a one or two year production cycle. It distributes fresh sports product from producers like MLB, NFL, and NCAA. It is constantly introducing new attractions at its theme parks. To continue its past success, Disney needs to pump out a steady stream of movie hits. Its recent movie blockbusters have raised the bar even higher, and Disney investors look for regular blockbuster hits from Disney. A series of subpar movies could depress its stock price.

- How well thought out and executed is your trial company's product portfolio? Which products are the current revenue generators (sometimes referred to as the "cash cows"), what are the replacement products to maintain that cash flow? What are the products of the future (the "rising stars") for growth of new revenues? Read the product and service discussions in the annual report of your trial company.

Disney added to its movie business by purchasing Pixar Animation Studios (*Toy Story*), Lucasfilm (the *Star Wars* and *Indiana Jones* movie franchises), and Marvel Entertainment (iconic comic book and movie characters). Disney built a new resort in Shanghai. Disney has cash generators in its ABC network and ESPN sports. Disney is actively developing new family-friendly products. For management's detailed discussion of

Disney's new product development find its annual report on its website.

- How well does your company manage its product distribution? A challenge for Disney is adapting to evolving channels of distribution for its entertainment services ESPN and the Disney Channel. Internet-based online video streaming is displacing older cable TV services, which had local monopolies and could charge higher fees which benefited Disney. To replace the revenue lost to cable cutting, Disney needs to create new subscription products around its ESPN and Disney Channel for distribution on lower-cost streaming services.

Brand

A *brand* is an imprint of a product on the customer's mind that sets an expectation. Brands imply reliability, consistency, and, for the most part, higher quality. Does your candidate company own a strong brand that draws customers? When you see a McDonald's restaurant anywhere in the world, the customer knows what to expect. A valuable brand name is trademarked to protect the unique identity of the product or company. You can immediately recognize many famous brand names old and new: *Nike, Apple, IBM, Hershey's Kisses, Sony, Twinkies, TWA, Corvette Stingray, Budweiser, Tiffany & Co.*, or *Bell Telephone*.

How well does your trial company maintain and manage its band? A brand can turn negative like the infamous "Ma Bell." That was the souring of a formerly valuable brand, as the company became associated with the evils of monopolistic business. Usually, a brand is corrupted when customer expectations are violated, such as by a drop in product quality or a breach of style.

Brands can be extremely valuable, especially when the brand becomes a more important component of a product's price than the good itself. In blind taste tests, different colas prove mostly indistinguishable, and people choose various unmarked colas as their preference. Yet, its customers are willing to pay a higher price for *Coca-Cola*. The *Coca-Cola* brand sets and meets an expectation of a specific taste that customers have come to expect of *Coca-Cola*. The *Coca-Cola* brand is so famous that it even has a nickname, *Coke*.

Disney is a world famous brand. With the *Disney* brand, parents trust and expect wholesome movie entertainment for their kids. In the *Disney* theme parks, they expect entertainment for the whole family in a clean, safe environment. Even more, families expect a *Disney* theme park vacation to produce lasting memories. The *Disney* brand is unique, no other entertainment brand comes close to it. Even *Coca-Cola* has a rival in *Pepsi*. And The Walt Disney Company owns a host of other valuable brands each with a large customer base: *ESPN*, *Pixar*, *Star Wars*, *Marvel*, and even *Mickey Mouse* and its many *princess* characters. These Walt Disney Company brands draw repeat customers.

Intellectual property and employee talent

Intellectual property (IP) is a company asset that comes from the inventiveness and creativity of people. Intellectual property includes inventions, literary and musical works, brand names, and designs. Examples of products with IP content are medicines, genetically modified foods, books, songs, technology products, and company logos. Much of the value of a high tech company is in it IP patent portfolio.

A company protects its IP by obtaining patents, copyrights, and trademarks that give it the exclusive right to use the invention or created work. A new patent is good for 20 years, a copyright for at least 70 years, and a trademark for 10 year periods which can be continually renewed. However, patents, copyrights, and trademarks are not absolute and can be lost through mismanagement or a court ruling. For example, aspirin, laundromat, and heroin were once trademarks that have become generic words. Patents on inventions can be challenged in court as an obvious idea or as prior art (previously thought of). You need to evaluate the risk inherent in your trial company's IP portfolio from lawsuits as well as from patent and copyright expiration. Does your trial company have new IP replacements under development?

While not formally classified as IP, your trial company also has valuable knowledge in its employees' expertise and know-how in manufacturing process, trade secrets, training methods, and teamwork. How talented and skilled is your trial company's labor force? How irreplaceable are your trial company's employees? How do they compare to the competition?

IP comes from talented people, whether as employees or independent artists. Patented inventions come from the scientists and engineers in research and development (R&D). Copyrights come from composers, designers, and writers. At your trial company how large is the R&D budget compared to its sales revenues, compared that of competitors? Who are the key creative people?

Disney has a huge IP foundation in its copyrighted films and the creative talent of its employees. They continue to design new theme park rides, build resorts, write movie scripts, and compose songs. Disney's talented employees create a steady flow of new IP ideas and new products.

Beating competitors

Competitors take away business that could have gone to your trial company. When you look for an investment in a particular industry, be it restaurant supplies or auto parts, you will need to look at all the competitors in the industry. Use these same methods to evaluate the competitors as you do evaluating your primary trial company. As you delve deeper into the industry, you will often discover a stronger company than your original trial company. You must be open to switching to that stronger company and researching it in place of your earlier trial company.

How does your trial company win against each of its competitors? What is the decisive advantage that your trial company wields against each competitor? Here are some factors that can decide who wins the competitive sale.

- Monopoly power: From owning exclusive patents, from large company economies of scale, or from marketshare dominance, monopoly power allows a company to charge more in a dominated market in order to charge artificially less and win sales in a targeted market.

- Political power: Favoritism or political influence in government regulations, contracts, or procurements
- Higher quality of products and services
- Lower prices from greater manufacturing expertise
- Customer loyalty and public goodwill built up over the years
- Superior sales force: Out selling and out negotiating the competitors
- Better availability of products: On store shelves, or direct delivery, or through production scheduling

In the consumer discretionary entertainment market, we find that Disney has arguably better movies for young audiences than its competitors. Disney has some dominance in sports programming through ESPN. Its theme parks have a good measure of public goodwill and customer loyalty. Its resorts and cruises seem comparable to those of its competitors and feature the Disney brand. It would be difficult to argue a Disney vacation is cheaper than its competitors' resorts or theme parks. Overall, we can conclude that Disney is a tough competitor in its markets.

Economic moat

A company has an economic moat when competitors face barriers to attacking its business or stealing its customers. Protective moats, also called barriers to entry, are a deepening of the competitive advantages that allow a company to win sales. Many of the advantages discussed above can form a protective moat to keep out new competitors. Examples of companies with deep protective moats include:

- Pfizer: Intellectual property in patents on drugs which provide a temporary monopoly
- Boeing: Design and manufacturing expertise in passenger jetliners

- Costco Wholesale: Large scale to offer lower prices than competitors
- The Coca-Cola Company: Customer loyalty to its world famous brand
- Taiwan Semiconductor Manufacturing Company: Investment base in expensive manufacturing equipment

What economic moat protects your trial company? Are the barriers long-lasting, can the moat be maintained? Patents expire after 20 years. Customer loyalty can be fickle. You must weight the long-term effectiveness of the moat. Pharmaceutical companies have a deep moat in drug patents that give them a monopoly on the drug until the patent expires, when overnight the moat evaporates and competitive generic versions of the drug become available. Are new patented drug coming to replace the lost sales revenues?

Disney's moat includes customer loyalty to its brands, the creative IP in its film portfolio, and its ESPN contracts with premier sports leagues and with cable companies. Many films in the Disney library are classics that can't be duplicated, and they will draw customers again in future rereleases. The ESPN sports contracts are subject to renewal at increasing cost; how will viewer habits changing away from cable channels to the internet affect ESPN? Customer loyalty among parents and kids to the Disney brand seems stable. I would characterize Disney's moat as long-lasting but relatively shallow. Competitive hit movies could draw away movie goers; competitor resorts can offer attractive vacation packages; a competitor sports network could bid for and win the broadcasting rights to the Olympics, the Superbowl, or the MLB World Series.

When investing for retirement income, you would prefer companies with a moat protecting the dividend stream you receive.

Economic engine

When you look for a company to invest in, you must identify and understand the *economic engine* creating value. Your trial company's economic engine is what puts money in your pocket. The economic engine should be straight forward and not mysterious once identified. You should be able to envision it working for you at your trial company, from making and selling the goods to the dividend payment flowing to you. For our purpose, an economic engine is not complete until it pays the dividend into your account.

Here are some basic economic engines; the best are reliable and profitable foundations for a business.

- Grow something and sell it: Farming, ranching, timber, flowers, fish farms
- Dig something up and sell it: Gold, oil, natural gas, metal ore, minerals
- Make something and sell it: Clothes, furniture, houses, boats, beer, shoes, art, books
- Collect a tax: Local, state, and national governments; union dues; membership fees
- Buy something and resell it for more: Wholesalers, distributors, retail stores, street vendors
- Rent out something: Apartments, cars, office space, canoes
- Gatekeeper usage charge: Toll roads, canals, shipping ports, airports, bridges
- Lend money and charge interest: Banks, financing companies, credit card loans
- Provide a service: Beauticians, lawyers, hospitals, colleges, entertainers, cellphone towers, country clubs
- Transport people or goods: Airlines, taxis, railroads, ships, oil and gas pipelines, post office
- Tap into a flow of money: Lottery operators, casinos, debit card and credit card transaction services, gift cards
- Communicate something: Newspapers, broadcasters, advertisers, writers, libraries

As the global economy has gotten more complex, so have its new economic engines. Verifying the economic engine is no longer a simple exercise. For example, very few people understand the inner workings of the worldwide web, commercially or technically. Many of the "dot-com" companies set up to exploit the internet failed because they couldn't create their economic engine, despite developing a working product. In the case of a biotech company, can you identify its economic engine? Can you name any drugs that it is selling to customers? Is the biotech company only an R&D company with a promise of future sales or license revenue?

Many people own Google stock, can you describe how Google makes money? What are all those Google software engineers working on? What product does Google sell—advertising? How does Google Maps or Google Gmail generate advertising cash flow? A key part of Google's complex economic engine is based on using the computing power and memory you buy within your personal computer or smart phone. Google's software on your device runs advertising applications to personalize that advertising exactly to your profile. Your spending on ever more powerful, faster PCs or smart phones supports Google's complex software, because Google uses the resources of your PC or smart phone to maximize their advertising revenue through your device. In the few seconds it takes for a webpage to download onto your smart phone or tablet, Google software will conduct an internet auction of the advertising space on your screen, with your personal browsing information, to the highest bidder for that space and download the auction winner's advertising targeted directly to you.

When you evaluate your trial company, you must research deeply to its core and figure out for yourself how its economic engine works. What you are ultimately investing in is the economic engine that powers the cash flow into your pocket.

A multi-division company like Disney has multiple economic engines. First, Disney *makes movies* that it *distributes* to theaters who *sell tickets* to customers. It operates theme parks, like Disney World, that provide the *service of entertaining vacations*, for which it *charges admission*. Disney *buys sports entertainment* and *resells* it via ESPN *subscriptions*. Disney *creates movie characters* and *licenses* them to toy manufacturers who *sell Disney toys*. You can visualize Disney's economic engines pumping money into its dividend to you.

Divisional cross-selling

When a company like Disney has several divisions, the divisions can help each other through cross-selling. A Disney movie success can spur the sales of *Frozen* princess dolls or *Star Wars* lightsaber toys. Disney sold countless recordings of the soundtrack to *Frozen*, and they created a *Disney on Ice* skating show version of *Frozen* to generate another round of ticket sales. Disney created theme park rides based on the *Cars* and *Star Wars* movies. Conversely, the *Pirates of the Caribbean* ride at Disneyland was the inspiration for the *Pirates of the Caribbean* movie franchise.

Cross-selling success can be lucrative. You should look for cross-selling synergies in the trial companies you evaluate. Is it a management objective? The large banks try to encourage their banking customers (checking, savings, and credit card) to use their in-house brokerage for investments, and they offer banking services to their investing clients. Your telephone company will try to win your internet, cable TV, and cellphone business to provide all your communications services.

Multi-division companies that don't have divisional synergies are candidates for breakup. Aptly described as conglomerates, their management attention is split between unrelated product lines. If the CEO came from one side of the company, she might not be adequately knowledgeable about the other businesses. Such companies might be more valuable broken up. In fact, some investors look for companies they think are likely to breakup with an increase in the overall value of the separated companies.

Company management

When you buy shares of a company through its stock, you are at the same time hiring the management team to run that company for you. As a potential part owner, you must evaluate the performance of the executive management and of the Board of Directors. The directors are elected by the shareholders, and they in turn hire the CEO (Chief Executive Officer) to run the company.

The Board of Directors will consist of the top executives of the company along with outside directors, who may themselves be CEO of another company or individuals accomplished in fields relevant to the company. The outside directors may also include representatives of major stockholders such as the company's founding family. A long-serving, successful CEO will nominate to shareholders outside directors who support him, and over time the CEO can come to dominate the board. What you look for in a board of directors is their ability to set the future direction of the company and give guidance to company management. Strong outside directors with independence from company management are generally desirable over yes-men directors controlled by the CEO.

The CEO is the most visible face of the company, apart from advertising figures. A good CEO is essential to the success of the company. The CEO must balance the need to control costs with the need to invest in new products, train employees, operate the business, and pay the dividend. A troubled company will often look to a new CEO to fix its problems, such as when Iacocca came in to rescue Chrysler, Gerstner revitalized IBM, or Jobs returned to save Apple.

How would you rate the performance of the management of your trial company? Read the management discussions in the annual report, check the comments of analysts from investment firms and brokerages. Is the management respected? Has the CEO position been unstable with high turnover?

Like many companies, Disney has had it ups and downs with its CEOs. As of this writing, the current management team under CEO Iger appears to be operating well. In our management evaluation here, we find that the biggest issue is the succession planning for the next CEO upon Iger's retirement. This is a common problem for companies: Do we want someone to continue executing Disney's current successful strategy or to anticipate and prepare for industry changes? The lack of a clear succession plan is cause for concern.

Financials

Reading company financial statements in annual reports is for the amateur usually the least fun part of investment research. However, if you like math puzzles, you might enjoy shifting through financial statements with your calculator or spreadsheet. If you plan to choose your own company stocks, whether as a hobbyist or a semiprofessional living on your investment income, you will need to understand the financial statements. I recommend that you take some finance classes (as opposed to accounting or bookkeeping classes) at your local college to get a grounding in the basics of analyzing financial statements. Over the years you can gain a comfortable understanding of the financial statements in the company's annual reports.

As you begin evaluating company financial statements, you can augment your own efforts by looking at the stock reports written by different analysts at brokerage firms for their assessment of your trial company's financial health. Generally, the analyst will compile a spreadsheet model spanning years of the company's financial data. They will look for year-by-year stability or changes in certain key financial ratios, and they will call out problems that they see, such as an increase in long-term debt or a shortfall in cash flow to support dividends.

In this age of the internet, you can find such spreadsheet models already compiled for you online. If you search for "Disney financial analysis" or "your-trial-company financial analysis," you will find websites such as those of *NASDAQ* and *Morningstar* with a wealth of prepared financial data for you to use in your evaluation. I suggest that you search these companies now to take a look and follow along in our discussion. However, these data sites do not replace reading the annual reports themselves for the management discussion of the financial statements, particularly the accompanying explanatory notes.

In beginning to analyze financial statements, focus first on your trial company's *debt* and on its *expenses*. The company's debt consists of its outstanding bonds and commercial bank loans. While what is considered a normal amount of debt varies considerably by industry, a higher debt load burdens a company by limiting its flexibility to spend cash to deal with other problems. Always, the less debt a company has the better. A sharp increase in debt is a red flag that must be examined to see how that debt will be repaid. A disproportionate increase in expenses is usually undesirable, unless it can be justified toward a good purpose like increased R&D, a new product rollout, or increasing production levels—activities that will generate new sales revenue. The first signs of trouble at a company are often reflected in increased expenses or debt to deal with that problem.

Next, look at the company's *cash flow*, which is not the same as *sales revenue* or *profit*. Cash flow is the movement of money in, through, and out of the company. Cash comes in when customers pay their bills (not when the sales revenue is recorded), cash goes out when the company pays its own debt and bills. The use of cash includes debt payments, expenses, buying raw materials, salaries, lease payments, and taxes. Your dividend is paid out of the remaining cash flow, not revenues, not profit. After all the cash in and cash out, the cash flow needs to be positive and the company's cash reserve account growing for the company to stay healthy. However, if cash flow is negative, then the company will have to use its cash reserve or take on more debt to make ends meet. Constant negative cash flow cannot be sustained and will be the death of the company.

A company's sales revenue and profit are the financial data most widely reported every quarter. You look for sales revenue to be increasing steadily, as that indicates the company is growing. You look for profit to be increasing, because that indicates the company will make money when it delivers the goods sold and the customer pays its bills. A positive cash flow indicates that sales are completed satisfactorily and the company is generally operating well. A regular, increasing dividend indicates the company takes care of its shareholders.

For Disney, in a cursory look at the time of this writing, we find that its debt has recently increased. This appears to be roughly offset by an increase in property and plant which may be from the investment in building a new theme park recently opened. Expense levels seem stable. The cash on hand has increased, so cash flow is trending positively. Key financial ratios are fluctuating in a narrow range or improving. Both revenue and profit are increasing. Disney's financial condition appears healthy. And most important for us, Disney has regularly increased its dividend.

Dividend history

The long-running dividend paid over the years is a tribute to a record of success and good management. The dividend history provides us confidence that your trial company is functioning well. This confirmation is not available for a company that does not pay a dividend, whether healthy or not. Particularly for the income investor, you should look for a dividend that has grown over the years. If a company was forced to reduce its dividend, which can happen even to good companies in a severe recession, how long until the company restored it dividend? You will learn later that the dividend is a complement to bond interest in an income portfolio.

As we discussed earlier, young companies that are growing rapidly likely will not pay a dividend, choosing instead to invest profits and cash flow in new product R&D, hiring and training new employees, and building a sales force to grow the company. For young companies, you can for a limited time substitute stock price appreciation for dividends. Ultimately, we look for growth companies who, as they mature, do plan to start paying a growing dividend. Examples are Intel, Microsoft, and Genentech which was acquired by Roche Holding Ltd. who pays a dividend.

You should be cautious of companies that are only concerned with growth. If a successful technology company grows by constantly replacing older products with new products, while never paying a dividend to its shareholders, one day its new product may flop and its stock price crash. The unrealized gains accumulated in the stock will vanish. Beware of companies that hoard cash instead of paying a dividend. Having excess cash often leads to poor decisions to use that cash, such as the ill-conceived acquisition. Any company that doesn't pay dividends nor grows its stock price is a poor investment.

Likewise, be cautious about companies paying outsized dividends yielding above six or seven percent. If a company runs into trouble, its stock price will react dropping quickly. However, the company management may not reduce its dividend immediately, hoping to reassure shareholders while waiting for a quick recovery. In this case the dividend yield could remain very high for a while, until the company runs out of cash and is forced to cut the dividend.

Dividend versus stock repurchase

Sometimes a company with an abundance of cash may choose to buy back its own stock on the open market rather than pay or increase a dividend. This is particularly true if the company is uncertain about sustaining its future cash flow, perhaps due to an aging product line or patent expiration. The cash may be a one time windfall such as from the sale of a subsidiary. In such cases the management may conduct stock repurchases which can be stopped at any time, rather than pay a dividend which can't be maintained.

A stock repurchase should reduce the number of outstanding shares. The value of the company will then be divided among fewer remaining shares, which makes each share more valuable. The dividend formerly paid on repurchased shares can be redirected to increase the dividend of the remaining shares. In theory, the more valuable shares, possibly with a higher dividend, should push up the stock price. Often, however, the repurchased shares are distributed to employees and executives as incentive stock. The stock repurchase and redistribution then really become a form of employee compensation. The cash is paid to the employees and executives rather than to the shareholders.

Share repurchases are only good for you, if they result in a higher dividend or stock price for your shares. Without a dividend increase you also loose the benefit of the compound earnings you could have had from reinvesting that dividend increase. You should track the use of repurchased shares to determine if the benefit accrues to you or to the employees and executives. Then you take that practice into account in your evaluation of your trial company.

Disney has had a regular stock repurchase program and a relatively low dividend. Disney appears to have taken opportunistic advantage of drops in its stock price, which it perceived to be temporary, to repurchase a large number of shares at a cheap price. However, there has been some criticism of its use of cash for stock repurchases vis-a-vis its low dividend payout.

Visit the company

You can visit Disney at the movies, in their retail stores, at their theme parks, on television, or at a Disney resort to investigate the company, its products, and its business practices.

You may be able to visit your trial company and see some things for yourself. If you are near their manufacturing facilities (perhaps while on your vacation), take any tour that the company might offer of its plants. A company may have a sales or service office near you, drop in if they allow visitors. Certainly go to see the stores of any retailer. Attend a public speech by an executive of the company. Watch interviews of its executives and key employees. Try to get a sense of the following:

- Do the employees seem to enjoy working there? What is the mood of the staff? Do you hear jovial conversations?
- Do they appear serious about their tasks? Do you see people wasting time? Do they appear stressed out?
- Are they proud of their product, their company, and their work?
- Is the office or factory organized? If it appears disarrayed, is it due to, say, the year-end rush, or does it appear to be chronic disorder?
- What is the attitude toward safety rules?
- Do they have adequate space, the latest equipment, or antiquated computers?

Any clue or impression may give you an insight into the company and help your investment evaluation.

Draw your conclusion: Can you invest in this company

If you have diligently gone through the evaluation steps we have described, you are ready to make a decision. You can be confident that you have covered the basics, that you have learned a lot about the company, and that your decision will be well considered. It's time to decide: Can you invest in this company? If yes, add it to your investable company short list. However, don't be disappointed if you are still undecided whether you want to buy your trial company, because that usually translates to "No, toss it out." You will reject many more companies than you find investable companies right for you. Move on to your next candidate company. However slowly your vetting process goes, be patient; you will not find the stocks for your portfolio all at once.

After you have studied a variety of candidate companies, rejecting many along the way, you will arrive at one or two companies to start with that you feel confident in. Over time as you research more companies, you will build a short list of companies that you want to invest in and gradually accumulate more shares of. This is how your stock portfolio begins.

Stock strategies and tactics

Now we turn our attention to how do you go about buying your selected companies. We will examine some of the popular methods of investing your money to see how to use them properly and which ones to avoid as a nonprofessional.

Long-term investing

Review our chapter on self-assessment, where we discussed the importance of taking the long-term view on investing. When you look at yourself, can you take the long-term path to investing? The following are long-term investing strategies and techniques you can use individually or in combination to buy stock in your selected company.

- *Buy-and-hold*: The classic time-honored strategy where you buy the stock of a large, well-run, financially solid, company and hold it as it pays you dividends (sometimes known as a *blue chip* company). Buy-and-hold is not the same as buy-and-ignore. You will regularly need to reassess the company to make sure its economic engine is running well, pumping money into your account. Buy-and-hold is a conservative, foundational strategy well-suited to be a part of every stock portfolio.
- *Dollar cost averaging*: We know that if you invest, say, $10,000 all at once in your selected company, the stock price could move up or down over the next days. If it moves down, you start with the handicap of an immediate unrealized loss. Dollar cost averaging is a purchasing technique you can use to avoid this poor start by placing several orders over time, say, buy $1,000 of shares every week for ten weeks. You will buy some stock batches at a higher price

and other batches at a lower price, with the overall price averaging somewhere in the middle. Dollar cost averaging your purchases has a second benefit that we will explain later in the section on buying mutual funds.

- *Dividend reinvesting*: Review the chapter on the power of compounding earnings. As you build up your stock portfolio, the dividend flow will accumulate as cash in your account. You must reinvest that dividend cash in additional shares of one of the companies you already hold or in the company that you are currently buying. The periodic reinvesting of dividends takes advantage of both compounding of earnings and dollar cost averaging.

- *Automatic reinvestment of dividends*: Some companies may have a dividend reinvestment plan (DRIP) whereby shareholders can automatically reinvest their dividends in additional shares of company stock held in a stock account at the company. DRIP programs allow the shareholder to buy fractional shares, which the company will keep track of and aggregate into full shares. Some brokerages may offer a DRIP, holding fractional shares in an account at the brokerage. Such dividend reinvestment plans are convenient and reinforce the compounding of earnings. However, you should be careful to keep track and not end up over time with too much money invested in any one company.

- *401(k) etc. investing*: The payroll deduction into a 401(k) or other retirement plan is a disciplined way to save and invest. Money is taken out of your paycheck and invested for you in the mutual funds you have chosen, automatically dollar cost averaging. At least once a year you need to review your 401(k) mutual fund selections. Be sure you contribute enough to get all of any matching contribution from your employer—it's free money!

- *Mutual funds and ETFs*: Mutual funds are intended to be a long-term buy-and-hold investment. The fund manager evaluates companies and buys and sells their stocks for you. Within the mutual fund you are diversified holding many selected companies, so you are not dangerously overconcentrated in just a few companies. While ETFs were created as a trading vehicle to track stock indices and stock sectors, they can also be used in a buy-and-hold strategy. The drawback (if it is such) is that no manager evaluates the individual fixed stocks in an ETF. If you don't want to select your own stocks, investing through mutual funds and ETFs is a viable alternative.

- *Employee stock purchase plan*: You should view an employee stock purchase plan as part of your employee compensation rather than as an investment plan. Participate in the stock purchase plan to get any employee discount or company matching contribution—the free money—but be careful about buying too much company stock. Be aware that employee stock purchase is doubly risky. If your company runs into trouble, you could be laid off while at the same time your company stock price crashes. So, you should evaluate your employer just like any candidate investment and determine how much company stock, if any, you want to own long-term. Then, when the vesting period is complete, you should sell any excess amount of your company stock and reinvest it in another stock in your portfolio.

When to sell in a long-term strategy

When you buy and hold high quality companies, you will need to do relatively little selling of your stocks. The weekly or monthly ups and downs in the stock price are usually insignificant. The time to sell any company will be when you see its essential competitive factors deteriorate. Regularly reexamine the company's economic engine, look for early warning signs the economic engine is weakening. In your periodic reevaluation you should see a market shift away from the company's products before they become obsolete (as film cameras did), or a management misstep resulting in a drain on cash flow and profit (such as a poorly executed acquisition), or an exodus of talented key employees.

Similarly, the time to sell a growth company is when its growth slows with no prospect for it to begin paying a dividend to you. The company may not be failing, but it could have stalled. You should reevaluate the fundamental factors we discussed earlier to judge if the company can resume its growth; if not, then it's time to sell.

Trading and short-term investing

The short-term holding period for investments is generally acknowledged to be anything less than one full economic cycle, typically up to six years. I think a more useful delineation is simply that long-term investing is based on giving the company's economic engine time to work making money for you. Short-term investing is focused on the movements of the stock price in order to try to make money by trading the stock. What is common to all short-term techniques is a focus on the stock price rather than on the company fundamentals that we discussed earlier.

The following are short-term strategies you will often read about in the media. Because these tactics regularly call for trades based on price movements, they provide bountiful fodder for media. If you want to play with these short-term trading techniques, you should do so separately in your hobby account. For your important money focus on your long-term investments. Some of these short-term techniques are used by professional investors to add leverage to their investment bets (and they do call them "bets"). *Leverage* is the ability to control more stock with less money invested than the full purchase amount.

- *Dogs of the Dow*: The widely followed Dow Jones Industrial Average (Dow) consists of 30 major U.S. companies selected to be an index of the overall stock market. The Dogs are those 10 companies of the Dow with the highest dividend yield (dividend/stock price) at the end of the year. They become Dogs mostly because their stock price has dropped during the past year. The premise is that the Dogs are solid blue-chip type companies and likely to recover the next year. So, you buy the Dogs based on their low price, manifest in the high dividend yield, and sell as each one comes off the Dogs list when its price recovers. The Dogs of the Dow is inherently a short-term trading technique, where you buy and sell within a year or two. A potential weakness in the strategy occurs when a Dog truly is a troubled company that falls off the Dogs list due to a dividend cut, and you sell at a loss when the price drops even lower.

- *Sector rotation*: Economists have observed that over the past century and a half the economy rises and falls in irregular business cycles of three to six years and longer in recent decades. Individual sectors, like home construction or vacation travel, also rise and fall in or out of phase with the business cycle. Analysts cut the business cycle into various stages, for example: early-recovery → expansion → full-employment → contraction → recession. In sector rotation, which is a form of momentum trend investing, a portfolio manager tries to time his stock trades to his prediction of the rise and fall of the next business cycle. The portfolio manager rotates between different sectors, buying stocks in one sector as it bottoms out while selling in another sector as it tops out. Various analysts prefer different sectors for each stage. An example of sector rotation is shifting to consumer discretionary and financial stocks in the early stages; to industrials, materials, and information technology stocks in the middle stages; to energy and consumer staples stocks in the late stages; and to healthcare, utilities, and telecommunications stocks in the recession stage. Sector ETFs now make it feasible for individuals to attempt sector rotation timing. Your challenge is to predict the peaks and bottoms of irregular business cycles, which, frankly, no one has done reliably, not even Federal Reserve economists. The trading of ETFs for sector rotation is just as susceptible to emotionally driven bad decisions as trading individual stocks.
- *Margin*: "Buying on margin" refers to a client borrowing money from his broker to buy stock. You will pay interest on the loan

amount. The margin is the amount of security equity value and cash that client must maintain in the account to secure the loan. Margin leverage is very risky because it amplifies the profit or loss from the stock trade. For example, you purchase 300 shares of stock at $20 per share for a total cost of $6,000. You borrow $3,000 on margin and add $3,000 in cash to pay for the stock. Your margin leverage allows you to buy 300 shares of stock instead of 150 shares with just $3,000 in cash. If the stock falls to $10 per share and you sell, you will collect $3,000 that you must use to repay the $3,000 that you borrowed. You will have suffered the loss of your entire $3,000 cash investment plus the interest that you had to pay. If at any time the margin in your account falls below the required minimum, your broker must issue a margin call to you demanding the deposit of additional margin in cash or securities. In the past, hedge funds and personal fortunes have been wiped out by margin bets gone bad.

- *Short selling*: In a margin account you can sell a stock before you buy it, establishing a short position. (You own a stock in a long position. You owe a stock in a short position.) In short selling, you borrow the stock on margin from your broker to sell, as you anticipate the stock price will fall. For example, you expect a poor earnings announcement to depress the stock price. At some point later, you will have to buy the stock to return it to the broker. The risk is if the stock goes up. When you short a stock, the proceeds from the sale plus an added margin amount must be maintained in your account. You will have to pay interest on the borrowed stock and pay any missed dividends to the lending broker. These costs must be recouped before you can make a profit. These high carrying costs make short selling a very expensive and risky strategy. Short selling is often pitched to beginners as a way to make money when the stock market falls. However, can you accurately predict which stock will fall, or when?

- *Limit order, stop order*: The limit order and the stop order are trader's tools that place a condition on your trade order. These include the limit order (intended to get a certain price), stop order (intended to limit a loss), and stop-limit order. For example, you believe WXYZ company stock, which is currently trading around $15, will go up. You want to buy on a dip in the price, so you place a buy limit order at $14 for WXYZ stock. Your order can only be executed at a price of $14 or better. With this buy limit order you attempt to get a better price on your buy trade, but the buy limit order can be risky and backfire. One backfire is missed opportunity. If WXYZ is trading around $15 when you place your order, it may never fall to $14 to trigger your limit buy order. Once the stock begins climbing as you anticipate, you will have missed the chance to purchase at $15. Another more serious backfire is that this limit order sets you up to take a loss. If you are wrong and WXYZ falls, your limit order will purchase WXYZ at $14 even as the stock falls to $9. You are better off just buying WXYZ at $15, making sure you can reap the potential gain as well as the potential loss. Every type of limit or stop order has a flip side backfire risk.

- *Technical analysis and charting*: Review our earlier discussion of technical analysis and charting. Since trading is based on buy and sell signals from volatile price movements, the frequent trading action from technical charts makes them a favorite among short-term traders.

- *Flipping*: A trader upon hearing news or a rumor about a company may anticipate a certain market reaction in the stock price. She will buy or sell a stock, wait for the price to move, and then sell or buy respectively, flipping the stock in hope of a quick profit. You will hear the expression "Buy the rumor, sell the news," which is a flipper's motto. It means act fast on hearing the rumor and then profit on the public's reaction to the news.

- *Buying the dividend*: Also known as *dividend chasing*, this flawed idea involves buying a stock just before the ex-dividend date, harvesting the dividend, and then selling the stock. This strategy doesn't work because the price of the stock will adjust down on the ex-dividend date to compensate for the dividend. Also, you will incur two transaction costs, one for the purchase and another for the sale.

Ultra-short-term trading and gambling

Ultra-short-term traders, such as day traders and option players, trade with extremely short holding periods and embrace many of the short-term trading tactics discussed above. They need deep pockets, enough money to ride out a streak of bad luck and enough so what they lose is not going to hurt them. Ultra-short-term traders are content with many small profits, so their money isn't tied up too long; they move on to the next trade.

- *Day trading*: Day traders will buy and sell a stock within a few days, or a few hours, or even minutes. They often rely on hapdictions from technical analysis and charts to guide their trades. As soon as their trade turns profitable, if it does, they will look to cash out. This high frequency trading is inherently very risky. Buying on margin or shorting stocks only magnifies the risk. Some traders search the internet for company news and rumors in order to flip their stocks.

- *Option trading*: Options are written with an expiration date, usually in three months, though some options can be longer. Option trading occurs within this very short lifespan. The premium, which is the price, of an option is a fraction of the underlying stock's price and changes in concert with the stock price. Ultra-short-term traders use options to leverage their bets, because an option allows them to temporarily control much more stock at a fraction of the cost of buying that stock. The traders hope that the stock price will move sufficiently for the option to be profitable before it expires worthless. We will discuss options in the next section.

- *Commodity futures trading*: These trades involve contracts for farm and ranch products such as cocoa, wheat, corn, coffee beans, cattle, and hogs; for minerals such as copper, gold, and platinum; or for oil and natural gas. Trading commodity futures is strictly for the professional. As an amateur you will be outgunned at every turn. If you want commodity exposure in your portfolio, use a commodity fund.

Game on

Ultra-short-term trading is a competition among players. You should think of ultra-short-term trading as a competition no different than a chess tournament, the NCAA basketball tournament, or a poker tournament. Because ultra-short-term trading results are hapdictive, the winners and losers will be spread out on a statistical distribution. There will be both winners and losers at ultra-short-term trading, but most will lose. Just as a few individuals can make a living at poker or betting the horses at the racetrack, some people may make a living at trading. However, ultra-short-term trading is a zero-sum game where a few winners just take money from the losers. It is not investing as I view it. Review your earlier self-assessment, do you have the risk-taking competitiveness of a winning poker tournament player?

Avoid penny stocks

You should avoid stocks selling for under $5 per share, known as *penny stocks*. Even for your hobby account, these companies are too risky. Penny stocks are usually not listed on the exchanges, so you don't have the protection of the exchange rules. The penny stock company might not be required to file financial reports with the SEC, so you won't have adequate information. Sometimes you will hear wild tips about a penny stock that is supposedly going to explode up in value. These penny stock tips are a staple of junk emails and internet websites. Just understand that the tipper is a paid promoter or a salesman trying to sell something like a newsletter. Sometimes the tip is a scam where the tipper has bought the stock and is try to start a rumor that will temporarily jack up the stock price so he can flip the stock and make a quick profit.

If you do find a penny stock that is listed on an exchange, you should be very cautious. A listed company will have fallen to penny stock status only because it is in serious trouble, resulting in the loss of much of the stock's value. The company may have needed to raise cash and issued many new shares of stock. The increase in the number of shares dilutes the ownership of the current shareholders. Each shareholder's proportion of the total stock will have shrunk. The additional shares tend to push the stock price down. It's a gamble whether the company can return to health or its stock price can recover to former levels.

Option

The *option* is a popular trading vehicle used by traders as a leveraged substitute for the underlying stock. One option allows the trader to control 100 shares of the underlying stock. Since the value of an option is based on the price of the underlying stock, the option is a type of derivative. The option is not issued by the underlying company.

What is an option

An option traded on the exchanges is a standardized contract between the option writer and the buyer, who is also known as the holder. The contract gives the holder the right to buy a stock from the writer or to sell a stock to the writer for a limited time, typically up to three months, until the expiration of the option contract. A *call option* gives the holder the right to purchase 100 shares of a stock from the writer at a set strike or exercise price. A *put option* gives the holder the right to sell 100 shares of a stock to the writer at a set price. For example, the buyer of one option listed as "BCDE Aug 28 call 2.94" will pay a premium of $2.94 per share which brings the option cost to a total of $294. When she chooses to exercise the option, she can buy 100 shares of BCDE at the exercise price of $28 per share, coming to $2,800 for the 100 shares. The option must be exercised before the August expiration date, which is a standard date each month on the option calendar when all options expiring that month will expire at the same time. The option premium moves up and down along with the underlying stock's price. The holder of an option can sell her option, or a writer can buy an identical option to what she sold, to close their respective positions.

Option risk

The option risk is very different for the writer versus the buyer. The risk for the buyer in our example is limited to only the premium she paid for the option; the most she can lose is $294 on the call option. The buyer of a call has an unlimited potential gain, as high as BCDE's price can go. The buyer of a put profits the most when the stock price drops to pennies, as in a bankruptcy, and she can sell nearly worthless stock to the writer for $28 per share. This high upside at low premium cost makes option buying popular among traders. When the stock price is above the call strike price or below the put strike price, the option is "in-the-money." Otherwise, the option is "out-of-the-money." The catch is when the underlying stock doesn't move enough to cover the premium. BCDE would have to rise above $30.94, before the call option is profitable, or BCDE would have to fall by more than the put option premium to be profitable.

The writer of an option stands in a much riskier position. She has as much downside as the buyer has upside. If BCDE stock rises to $35 per share, the call option buyer can choose to exercise the call to purchase the stock at $28 from the call writer. The writer must procure the stock at $35, suffering a $7 per share loss, which is a $700 gross loss on the 100 shares. When combined with the $294 premium the writer received for selling the option, her net loss is $406. Similarly, if BCDE stock falls to $22, the put buyer can choose to exercise and force the put writer to buy BCDE at $28, when it is only worth $22. The writer suffers a $600 gross loss, offset somewhat by the premium amount received from selling the put.

Expiration and time value

When the option expiration date nears, in-the-money buyers will sell their option to close their position and take their cash. The option writer who had the stock price move against her, needs to buy back an identical option to close her position or face the exercise of the call or put she sold. An options writer would not want to sell a stock she doesn't own or buy a stock she doesn't really want, so it's preferable to close the position before expiration. Being subject to a call or put exercise would require a large amount of cash to follow through with the actual stock transaction.

Holders of out-of-the-money options can only watch them expire worthless, with the loss of the option premium.

In fact, most options expire worthless out-of-the-money. That is the reason option writers are willing to take the risk of a large loss. They expect the premiums collected from the many expired options to exceed any losses from having to buy back the few in-the-money options. The option writer has time on her side as the clock ticks to expiration; meanwhile, the holder can see the time value of her option erode each day. (The option's premium equals the in-the-money amount, if any, plus the time value to expiration.) For the buyer, the stock price must move favorably far enough, soon enough, to make up the purchase premium before any profit.

Covered call writing

We have described how selling options can be very risky. Selling a basic option is referred to as selling a "naked" option. However, if in the previous example the writer already owns 100 shares of BCDE and sells one call option, then she is "covered." If BCDE's price shoots up to $96, she is protected by having those 100 shares available to fulfill a call. She will lose the potential $6,800 gain that would have been hers if she had been able to keep the stock. However, she won't be forced to buy the stock at the very high cost of $9,600 to turn around and sell for $2,800 to the call holder. Alternatively, the writer could choose to buy an identical option at a very high premium near $6,800 to close her option position and keep her stock.

Similarly, the writer of one put option at a strike price of $28 can cover the put by depositing in her account $3,000 in treasury bills. In the event the put is exercised, the treasury bills cover the $2,800 cost to buy 100 shares of BCDE.

Covered call writing is often suggested as a way to boost the income from buy-and-hold stocks. For example, a call writer owns 300 shares of BCDE stock which pays a quarterly dividend of $.19 per share. The writer could sell three covered call options maturing in two months at a strike price that she thinks will likely be out-of-the-money. If she can get a premium of $.13 per share for a call option that eventually expires unexercised, she will have boosted her income to $.32 per share. Each quarter she can repeat selling three covered calls to boost her income.

Conventional wisdom describes covered call writing as a conservative option strategy, because you are protected from a big price move up. However, that is also its main fault: Your stock's biggest moves up will be called away, while you keep all the downside risk. Stock prices move unpredictably in the short-term, and much of a long upward trend will happen in quick spurts up, mixed with quick drops down. Covered call writing sets you up to lose the big gains, while suffering all the big loses. For this reason, I don't recommend covered call writing in a long term strategy.

Option as a tool

The option is a versatile short-term tool with many uses. In addition to the trading of naked options or covered calls, here are some other option tactics that individual investors and traders use:

- *Insurance put*: In certain situations a put option can be used to protect yourself temporarily against a fall in the price of a stock that you are holding and want to keep. For example, you hold LMNO biotech company that will announce next month the clinical trial results for an important new drug. If the drug fails, you anticipate the stock price will plummet, or if the trial results are very strong, the price will jump up. The company has other promising drugs, so you want to keep the company. In this situation, you might consider buying LMNO put options with a strike price close to the current stock price as insurance for your stock. (Remember, you will need one option for every 100 shares of stock.) If the stock price subsequently does fall, the put option premium will go up, because the put options allow you to sell your stock at the higher strike price. You can then sell the put options to recover in cash the value that you lost in the stock you hold. This use of an insurance put allows you to keep the stock without suffering the price drop. If the stock price goes up, then the put options will be out-of-the-money, and the purchase premium will have been the cost of the insurance protection.

- *Straddle*: In the example above, a trader, while not owning LMNO stock, may still try to profit from the pending announcement. If the trader believes the stock will react with a very big move up or down to the news good or bad, he can speculate with an option straddle that covers both possibilities. He would buy a call on LMNO and also buy a put on LMNO, both with the same strike price near the current market price of LMNO stock and with the same expiration date. If LMNO moves up, the call makes money, or if LMNO moves down, the put makes money. The high risk for the trader is that he will have to recover two premiums, one for the call and one for the put, before the straddle can make a profit, hence the need for a big price move. If the reaction is muted and doesn't move LMNO's stock price enough, he will lose money.

- *Protective put*: Similar in principle to an insurance put, the protective put is used by traders to lock in temporarily a large unrealized gain in a stock. The put protects against a fall in the price of the stock, while the trader hopes for further gain.

- *Custom return profiles*: Option traders can mix two, three, or four options to form various risk/return configurations, the straddle being one example. Of course, there will be two, three, or four premiums to recover before any profit. As discussed previously, these ultra-short-term tactics seem closer to gambling than to investing. However, in the hands of a skilled professional investment product designer, one year and longer options can be combined with bonds to create structured products with very conservative or very aggressive risk profiles. (See the previous discussion of structured products.) These preconstructed products are sold to investors as a single, unified structured product.

The use of options in combination with stock makes the income tax calculation complicated. You should consult with your tax professional.

How to select and buy bonds

You can use bonds for many purposes. People buy short-term bonds to hold money they will need within a few years. With a bond they know the principal will be there at maturity, unlike stocks which can fall in value. People buy bonds for safe and steady income in retirement. Also, people buy bonds to balance the risk in their overall portfolios, as we will discuss in the section on building your portfolio. Your purpose for the bond will determine the bond characteristics you look for.

Buying bonds is very different from buying stocks. This is because no two issues of bonds are alike. Bond are issued, even if by the same company or municipality, with differing coupon rates, maturity dates, bond ratings, seniority, and legal covenants. There are no bond exchanges, like stock exchanges, to provide a ready marketplace for bonds.

You will buy bonds mostly through your broker. Your broker will offer you bonds from its own inventory, or, if you are looking for a specific bond, such as one from a nearby school district, your broker will search through its sources.

An exception is that you can buy treasury bonds directly from the U.S. Treasury by opening an account through their website. However, at the time of this writing, if you want to sell that treasury bond before it matures, you will need to transfer it to your brokerage account in order to sell it.

When you wish to sell a bond, your broker could buy it into inventory or will put it out for bids from buyers. Some older, obscure bonds may be difficult to sell and then only at a heavy discount and not quickly.

Determine what you need in a bond

Review the earlier discussion of bond rating, bond maturity and call, and tax-advantaged municipal bond.

When you buy a bond, you will need to specify to your broker certain parameters for the bond. These parameters follow from the purpose you have in mind for the bond. For example, if you are planning to pay college tuition with the money in the bond, that will determine in large part the maturity of the bond you buy.

Your first decision is whether you should buy tax-free municipal bonds or taxable corporate bonds. As discussed previously, tax-free municipal bonds typically have a lower yield than comparable corporate bonds and appeal mainly to people in high income tax brackets. You will need to consult with your tax advisor to determine which makes sense in your tax situation. If you are vulnerable to the alternative minimum tax, you should tell your broker you want a municipal bond that is not subject to the AMT. Some folks just don't like paying income tax, so they will choose tax-free bonds and sacrifice a bit of yield.

Safety is a primary appeal of bonds, and you will want to specify the minimum bond rating (that is the maximum risk) you can accept, for example an **A** rated bond. Generally, you should stick with investment grade bonds, which are **BBB** or higher. Someone with extensive bond experience and a large bond portfolio may wish to augment his portfolio's yield with a small allocation to riskier below-investment-grade bonds, for example a **C** rated junk bond. For the new or small investor, investing in junk bonds is best done through a high-yield bond mutual fund which is broadly diversified.

You should discuss with your broker the possibility you might want to sell the bonds quickly to reinvest or for a cash emergency. You may want a bond for which there will always be ready buyers to provide you liquidity. These would be bonds from blue chip companies and large thriving municipalities. You would exclude some higher yielding though obscure bonds that could take weeks to sell.

You should determine a target yield, based on your income needs, that you would like to get from the bond. It is not enough just to say "the highest yield or interest rate," as those would be from junk bonds. Your target yield will affect both the risk and the maturity of the bond. Your desired target rate may not be attainable at an acceptable level of risk.

The maturity you specify for a bond will be influence by several interrelated factors. Longer maturities typically garner higher yields. The relationship between yield and time to maturity is known as the *yield curve*. The shape of the yield curve fluctuates with the prevailing interest rate at each maturity, to which bond yield and price are equated. The prevailing interest rates are driven by market forces and by Federal Reserve actions and policy. Interpreting the yield curve requires a sophisticated understanding of interest rate history and dynamics, as well as insight into the possible future direction of interest rates.

When you go to your financial advisor with your bond parameters, he will help you interpret the current yield curve and find a recommended selection of bonds with the maturity, yield, and other characteristics suited to your needs. He will help you evaluate them and choose a bond.

Evaluating corporate bonds

The fundamental analysis of a company for its corporate bonds is the same as the process we discussed for its stock. Only the emphasis is different. The bond analyst will focus more on the company's cash flow that will pay interest and repay the bond principal, as well as pay its stock dividend. How sustainable is the cash flow? Will there be sufficient cash for the company to redeem its bonds upon maturity? Or, will the bonds need to be refinanced with a new replacement bond issue? Will there be extra cash so that the company might recall its bonds before maturity? As we discussed, an early call of your bond is likely undesirable for you.

Additionally, the bond analyst will review the covenants in the bond *indenture*, which is the originating contract document when the bond is issued. The covenants are complex and written in legalese. She will look at pledged assets, if any, and at the bond's seniority versus other company bonds. The covenants could contain emergency triggers of clauses meant to protect the company, which in turn adversely affect the bondholder.

As a practical matter, most individual investors rely on the bond agency's rating as a substitute for doing this analysis themselves. For them, the investment grade rating confirms the bond's safety. For you, the bond rating can augment your own evaluation of the company.

Evaluating municipal bonds

Recall that municipal bonds come in two types: general obligation bonds supported by taxes, and revenue bonds supported by a specific income source.

To evaluate a general obligation bond, the bond analyst will examine the tax base. For a new school district bond, she will look at the assessed valuation of the real estate in the district, the property tax rate, and the other bonds supported by the same property tax dollars. She will look at the stability of property values, tax payment delinquencies, and tax revenue growth to model the future tax revenue that will support the new bond and existing bond obligations, as well as the operation of the schools. For a city bond, the analyst will also look at the sales tax and other tax revenue that the city receives. She will look at the affluence of the community and the city's population growth.

For a revenue bond, the bond analyst will examine the revenue source. For a hospital bond, examining the business of the hospital will be similar to evaluating a company for a corporate bond. For a toll road or bridge, she will look at the strength of the local economy that will determine the commercial and commuter use of the toll road or bridge that generates its revenue. The revenue must support the operation and maintenance of the enterprise with enough left over to service the bond obligations.

Here as well, most individual investors rely primarily on a bond agency's rating. You should discuss with your financial advisor the trade-offs in buying uninsured municipal bonds versus insured municipal bonds, both having the same rating.

Bond strategies

Buy-and-hold

When you buy bonds for interest income, you will naturally be buying and holding. At first, you might want to by a bond with the highest yield for the highest income, which generally implies the longest term bonds. However, when the prevailing interest rates are running lower historically, you don't want to lock yourself in with a 20-year bond at today's rates, only to see the rates go higher in a few years and remain higher. You obviously will have missed a lot of income. Selling the 20-year bond is not a satisfactory solution, as its price will have gone down as prevailing interest rates went up. (You will recall from earlier chapters that bond yields generally increase with longer maturities, that bond prices go down when prevailing interest rates go up, and that municipal bonds have lower yields than comparable taxable bonds due to their favorable tax-free status. Revisit Table 3 Example of bond spreads for ten-year bonds.)

So what is the thought process buy-and-hold bond buyers use in selecting bonds? As we discussed above, you first determine the parameters for a bond that meets your need. Let's say, for this example, that you determined you want an investment-grade, tax-free municipal bond to lower the risk profile of your portfolio. (The selection process will be the same for a taxable bond.) Your financial advisor or bond broker will identify a selection of bonds that meet your parameters. Table 4 shows a sample yield curve for your state's municipal bonds on any given day when you might seek to buy a bond. Experienced bond buyers and their brokers look at the tradeoff between the added increment of yield and the extra year to maturity. In other words, are you willing to buy that extra increment of yield by paying for it with an added year to maturity? In Table 4, you will see that the yield curve is not smooth but bumps along higher due to the specific bonds offered for any maturity year. The yields vary in each maturity year because of the different bond issuers and bond ratings. In some cases, a highly sought after bond may come to market, resulting in a lower yield for that maturity year.

Table 4 Example of a municipal bond yield curve

Years to maturity	Yield %	Incremental yield % for additional year
1	.960	---
2	1.063	.103
3	1.149	.086
4	1.188	.039
5	1.381	.193
6	1.509	.128
7	1.543	.034
8	1.925	.382
9	1.955	.030
10	2.135	.180
11	2.210	.075
12	2.495	.285
13	2.387	-.108
14	2.628	.241
15	2.759	.131
16	2.710	-.049
17	2.792	.082
18	2.805	.013
19	3.279	.474
20	2.824	-.455
21	3.145	.321
22	2.117	-1.028
23	2.651	.534
24	3.366	.715
25	3.284	-.082
26	3.128	-.156
27	3.225	.097
28	3.617	.392
29	2.845	-.772
30	3.878	1.033

If you study this yield curve, you can see that the increments to yield increase, albeit unevenly, for additional years to maturity through the 15-year bond. For 16-year bonds and longer, the increments flatten out becoming smaller on average. This is a normal yield curve, which rises steeply in the early years and flattens out in the long maturities. The longer maturities have the higher yields overall, but gain in much smaller yearly increments. Where the yield curve bends to flatten out is sometimes called the "sweet spot," in this example around year 15. With this particular yield curve, I suggest that you look at bonds up to 15 years of maturity. On this rising portion of the yield curve, for every year added to the bond's maturity you will get a steep increase in the bond's yield. Out on the flatter, longer portion of the yield curve, every additional year will get you little additional yield. All else being equal, you can chose between the 12-year bond or the 15-year bond. These two bonds give you the best trade-off of incremental yield for extra years of maturity. There is no need to lock yourself unnecessarily into a longer maturity.

Note, however, that bond yields can swing widely along with changes to the prevailing interest rates. At extreme times, you should be flexible and judiciously adjust your bond strategy. If 20-year or 30-year bond interest rates are at historic highs and likely to come down to historic norms, then it would make sense to buy even 30-year bonds to lock in that very high interest rate for many years of income. Conversely, if interest rates are at historic lows, it makes sense to buy very short-term bonds so that when they mature in a year or two you can reinvest the funds at a higher interest rate. It may even make sense to avoid bonds and buy a dividend-paying stock with a little higher risk.

Managing bond maturity for availability of cash

Review the previous discussion of bond liquidity.

Investment grade bonds are often used to set aside money for a future expenditure, because you can depend on the timely return of the principal at maturity, while earning interest in the meantime. One of your chief tasks when planning bond purchases is to make sure your money becomes available when you need it. You don't want to have to sell your bond before its maturity, as you could suffer a realized loss.

The most straight forward method is to time your bond maturities to match anticipated expenditures. So if you will have college tuition expenses to pay in five years, you can buy bonds that mature in five years. If, when you retire in seven years, you plan to buy a boat or recreational vehicle, you can buy bonds that mature in seven years to have funds for your anticipated purchase.

The drawback to matching bond maturity to expenditure is that you miss getting a higher yield, if you could have bought bonds with a longer maturity. The bond ladder and bond barbell strategies address this problem.

Bond ladder

With a little advanced planning you can implement a *bond ladder* that will earn higher yields. Let's say you want to set aside money for four years of college tuition for your child. Instead of waiting until five years before college as in the previous example, you plan earlier to buy bonds in the sweet spot of the yield curve, which might be, say, around 11-year bonds. Then 11 years before the first year's tuition, you buy an 11-year bond to cover the first year's tuition. The next year you again buy an 11-year bond for the second year's tuition. Similarly, you buy 11-year bonds for the last two years of college tuition. You end up with a sequence of four 11-year bonds in a short bond ladder. Each bond is a rung on the ladder that will mature as funds are needed to pay each year's tuition. The 11-year bonds will earn you a higher yield than the shorter 5-year bonds, giving you higher interest income.

A bond ladder can make some funds available each year while still earning higher yields. Let's say you have $238,000 in a stock portfolio that you want to reinvest in bonds for retirement income, and the sweet spot has moved out to around 14-year bonds. You don't want to purchase one $238,000 bond that will lock up your principal for 14 years, as you want money available should you need it. Instead, you can implement a bond ladder. Each year you sell stock and by a $17,000 bond maturing in 14 years. Buying bonds yearly, over time you will build a ladder with 14 bonds of $17,000 each. Thereafter, each year a bond will mature making $17,000 available to reinvest in another bond or to spend as needed. By reinvesting each year's maturing bond in a new 14-year bond, you can extend the bond ladder indefinitely.

A bond ladder has another advantage, too. As prevailing interest rates fluctuate, stepping into a bond ladder one bond per year will dollar cost average your purchases so you won't be caught purchasing all your bonds at a low interest rate and high price.

A bond ladder can take patience to set up, however you are rewarded with your bonds yielding higher interest.

Bond barbell

Certain situations call for a *bond barbell* strategy. A bond barbell has very long-term bonds balanced with very short-term bonds with nothing in the middle. Previously, we gave the example where the prevailing interest rate is extremely high at the long end near the 30-year bonds and likely to come down to normal. In this extreme case, you would do better buying 30-year bonds to lock in the extreme yields. In order to preserve some availability of funds, you can balance the very long bonds with short one-year or two-year maturity bonds that you continually rollover. The result is a bond barbell with very long bonds providing high yield and very short bonds providing availability of cash. The two ends do not need to be the same size. The amount invested at short end will be based on your anticipated cash needs, and the amount at the long end will be as much as you can comfortably lock up for so long. You can consider a bond barbell whenever the long-term yields are very high.

As years go by and as prevailing interest rates return to normal levels, you invest new money in mid-term bonds to fill in the rungs and move the barbell toward a bond ladder.

Zero-coupon bond

A type of bond that you can use to match a bond payout to a future cash need is the *zero-coupon* bond. A zero-coupon bond pays no interest during the life of the bond, instead the bond is sold at a discount to the par value that will be paid at maturity. For example, if you want to receive $10,000 at maturity in twelve years and the prevailing interest rate is 3%, you could buy a zero-coupon bond today at the discounted price of $6,995. This has the advantage of requiring a smaller upfront cash outlay than a regular bond. All of the earnings at the imputed 3% rate goes forward to the one payout at maturity. Because zero-coupon bonds pay no periodic interest, they are not suitable for those who need current income.

Kicker bond

Review the discussion of bond maturity and calls.

Some experienced bond investors look for *kicker bonds* to potentially boost their portfolio's yield. A callable bond may be priced for the first call date with its lower yield to call. When such a bond is not called early, you get the bonus of the higher yield to maturity, which is the "kick." Potential kicker bonds can be identified by comparing the yield to maturity, which will be higher, to the yield to call. However, you should allow for a kicker bond being called and expect the lower yield to call to be your likely return.

The possibility of a call complicates using kicker bonds in a bond ladder or barbell strategy. The calling of a bond will leave a hole in your bond ladder or barbell. You will likely not be able to find a replacement bond with the higher yield you lost. You should consult with your financial advisor about the call risk in using kicker bonds in your bond strategy.

Leave bond trading to the professionals

The individual bond trader can not hope to compete with the institutional bond traders. They have too many advantages, including mainly one of scale. They trade millions of dollars in bonds to make a slim profit margin, which they can do over and over to accumulate gains. The magnitude of their trades spreads out their trading costs over thousands of bonds. Meanwhile, the individual trader's gains, if any, would be reduced by his trading costs. Additionally, the professional trader, investing hundreds of millions of dollars, has the sophistication to exploit kinks in the yield curve.

The cost of buying or selling bonds is included in the offer or bid price you are quoted for the bond. You will not be quoted prices as favorable as those offered to professional traders with their tremendous volume of trades. We will discuss trading costs further in a discussion on fees and costs.

You as an individual bond investor should focus on building a diversified bond portfolio to hold for the interest income.

Bonds through mutual funds and ETFs

A viable alternative to buying your own bonds is to invest in bonds through mutual funds or ETFs. Even for a small investment, the mutual fund or ETF can provide you diversification across many different bonds. The bond analysts at an actively managed mutual fund will do their own evaluation of a bond to validate the bond rating from the agencies. Review our discussion of bond mutual funds and ETFs.

The key disadvantage of bond mutual funds and ETFs is that, unlike individual bonds, they don't have a maturity date when the bond principal will be repaid to you. So to raise cash you will have to sell shares of the mutual fund or ETF at the market price, taking a realized loss or gain. You can not depend on the return of your investment principal as cash on a definite date.

How to select and buy mutual funds and ETFs

Many of the steps in selecting a mutual fund or an ETF are similar, so we will discuss them together. In the following sections, we will be referring to both mutual fund and exchange-traded fund when we say the "fund." We will say "mutual fund" or "ETF" when we mean only one or the other.

Bear in mind mutual funds are designed to be a buy-and-hold investment. ETFs can be used both for a buy-and-hold strategy or for trading. Our discussion here will focus on selecting funds for the long term.

Selecting fund styles

Review the earlier discussion of mutual fund styles and ETF styles. Your first step is to determine the style of fund for your needs. For your very first fund, I recommend a U.S. domestic large-cap growth fund. This style will invest in large companies having good growth potential. It will provide a foundation for you to build upon when adding funds with other styles.

Since you can buy funds with a relatively small initial investment, you can quickly begin to add more styles, while allocating money to each style. When you start to build your portfolio of funds, as in a 401(k) account, I suggest that you add funds with styles as outlined in the following order:

1. U.S. large-cap stock growth
2. U.S. small-cap stock growth
3. U.S. large-cap stock income or dividend-paying
4. U.S. intermediate-term corporate bond—investment grade
5. International large-cap stock growth
6. U.S. long-term corporate bond—investment grade
7. U.S. mid-cap stock growth
8. Targeted sectors—healthcare, technology, industrials, consumer discretionary, etc.

This set of fund styles, or some variation of it, would be a diversified portfolio for you. (We will discuss building your portfolio and diversification in more depth in a later section.)

As you gain experience investing with funds, you can adjust the fund styles listed above to suit your situation. There are no hard-and-fast rules for selecting funds, however, here are some guidelines for you to consider as your fund portfolio grows:

- When you are young and have a long time horizon, emphasize growth stock styles.
- As you near retirement, place a greater emphasis on income from stock dividend and bond interest styles.
- Usually, buy only one fund in any style, except perhaps two funds in the U.S. large-cap growth style.
- You can substitute a value, blend, or core stock style for up to a third of the amount in a growth stock style.
- A passive S&P 500 fund fits in the U.S. large-cap growth style.
- After U.S. large-cap growth, as you add funds, you don't need a fund in every style in the list above.
- After the initial funds, limit any one fund to no more than 20% of your total portfolio.
- You can invest different amounts of money in the different styles.
- In taxable accounts you can substitute tax-free municipal bond funds for the corporate bond funds.
- Be aware that many big mutual funds with a U.S. style, nonetheless, include an allocation of foreign stocks.
- Examine the holdings in each of your funds to avoid too much duplication in their holdings
- Ask your financial advisor to run a *correlation matrix* of your selected funds and explain the results to you. (A correlation matrix examines how much your funds move up and down in unison.)

I suggest you start with this straight forward approach to investing with funds. You may notice that for long-term investing I favor the growth style for stock funds. When we discuss building your portfolio in a later chapter, we will show how to balance the growth funds with individual dividend-paying stocks or with value style funds. We will also discuss a computerized model for selecting and weighting fund styles known as asset allocation.

You will undoubtedly encounter many more styles of funds, but do not be confused by them. Investment companies have created thousands of mutual funds and ETFs with all sorts of imaginative styles to appeal to every investor taste and fad. Just choose basic fund styles like those above that fit your plans. Avoid exotic style funds.

Hiring mutual fund managers

In choosing a mutual fund within a style, the nature of your investment decision is fundamentally different from choosing which stock or bond to buy. Instead of evaluating the business prospects of an individual company and its stock and bonds, the mutual fund decision becomes a hiring decision. You are hiring a manager to make your stock or bond selections for you. It's no different than hiring any other employee, choosing a doctor, or finding a remodeling contractor for your house. You look for the best performing portfolio manager and analyst team, just as you would hire the most productive employees, go to the most skilled doctors, or use a reliable remodeling contractor. In hiring your fund manager, the most important thing to look at is their long-term performance track record, both at their current fund and at any previous funds where they worked. Over the last five and ten years have they done well for their shareholders compared to other mutual fund managers with the same style?

The basic performance data you need can be found in the annual reports available on the mutual fund's website. You also need to read the manager's discussion of his results. What is his thinking on the performance of individual company selections? Is he sticking with his strategy and convictions, how confident is he? Is he making sensible adjustments to his strategy, correcting any problems? Do you agree with his assessment of his results?

Two prominent rating services are available to help you: Morningstar and Lipper. Morningstar is the source of the "5-star" rating system frequently quoted in media and advertising. Both companies sell data, performance metrics, and their rating of mutual funds to paid subscribers. Your financial advisor likely has access to one or both of these services, and you might also inquire at your local public library to see if they provide access to these services. Both services rate mutual funds and their managers on a scale of 1 lowest to 5 highest, though their methodologies differ. Most people simply look for a "5-star" rating in choosing a mutual fund. However, as you gain experience reading their reports, you will be able to discern their preferences or leanings in their reports. By weighing their reports along with your own year-by-year tracking of the manager, you will decide: Would you hire this manager?

As you study mutual fund managers, you will often hear the names of "famous" fund managers, "stars" in the industry as it were. When you do, you should not jump on their bandwagon. Many times these managers are featured in their company's advertising based on a recent outstanding year or two. They are getting a flash of public-relations-generated media attention. Instead, base your judgment on their long-term five and ten year performance record.

Tracking mutual fund managers

Evaluating mutual funds, means keeping track of individual managers as they move through their careers. If a successful manager leaves a famous fund, his track record walks out the door with him. You will want to reevaluate that famous mutual fund without his services.

Some large mutual fund companies will regularly shuffle their portfolio managers. For example, a new portfolio manager just promoted from being a successful analyst will be tried out with a small fund to manage, perhaps a sector fund in his specialty. If he does well, he will be reassigned to a larger, more important (to the mutual fund company) fund. This career progression rewards the manager who performs well and attracts new shareholder money to his fund. This process works very much like a baseball farm system with ballplayers advancing through the levels of the minor leagues to the major leagues, in this case from minor-sized to major mutual funds. Learn the names of your favorite portfolio managers and keep track of them, just as you might young baseball prospects through the farm system and via trades. You can get to know them, grow confident in their success, and then invest with them.

Tracking the careers of managers over the years, albeit a long process, is the key to mutual fund investing.

An opportunity arises when a successful manager you have been tracking, leaves to start a new mutual fund. You will be able to invest at the ground floor with a manager with a record of success. With a new small fund, the manager will be able to concentrate on buying his best stock ideas, unlike at a very large fund which can hit a limit on the percentage it can own of a smaller growing company.

Another opportunity you should track is a mutual fund run by a manager you like that has closed to new investors. When that fund reopens to new investors, you can buy into it before it closes again. The funds of the best performing managers will often be flooded with money from investors, so much so that the manager can not invest the money fast enough. In that case, such a fund will close to new investors, turning away clients sometimes for years. Those lucky enough to own shares of the fund will have a great manager working for them. You should keep track of closed mutual funds that you want to invest in, waiting for a reopening.

You may discover that you prefer evaluating managers of mutual funds over evaluating companies, stocks, and bonds.

Selecting an index mutual fund and ETF

Review the section on active management versus passive index fund. If you decide to invest in part or entirely with passive index mutual funds or ETFs, you will first need to determine the fund styles to include in your portfolio. For each fund style, you select a representative benchmark index which will list the stock or bond holdings that the passive fund will track. For example, in large-cap growth stocks you could choose, perhaps, the S&P 500 index or the Russell 1000 Growth index, among others. Though they are in the same style, the two indices will perform somewhat differently, because their stock holdings and methodologies differ. You can read about each index on its website and compare their list of companies. If you select a fund style that represents a specific industrial sector, you may find that the available indices can differ substantially in their list of stocks. This is because the stocks in any index are selected by an editorial board that acts in essence as the portfolio manager when the index's stock list is updated.

When selecting a passive fund for a style, you should look for an established fund with the highest return. By an established fund, I mean one from a major investment company that gives you confidence in its longevity and reliability. ETFs usually have lower total expenses than index mutual funds, so you would look to ETFs over index mutual funds with the same benchmark index.

Though a set of ETFs may be in the same style, they may track different indices. Look for the ETF in that style with the highest return. Even funds tracking the same benchmark index may have differences in their individual performance due to differences in their expenses and how they handle dividends and interest. ETFs are set up using various legal struc-tures which affect the timing of reinvesting dividends and interest, which results in performance differences.

However, if you plan to use sector rotation or frequently reallocate assets with index funds, then you might consider index mutual funds all in the same fund family. You can usually switch between index mutual funds within a fund family with no sales charge. Implementing the same strategy with ETFs would incur sales charges for each sale and purchase. In an active allocation or rotation strategy, you will need to include the ETF sales charges in the cost comparison to index mutual funds in one family.

You may hear the term *tracking error*, which is a measure of how closely a fund tracks its benchmark index. While this is a useful metric for evaluat-ing index funds, for our purposes it is overshadowed by the highest return.

Fund family

Any mutual fund or ETF that you research likely will belong to a *fund family*. A fund family is the brand of the investment company sponsoring the fund. Even those funds that are famous by themselves are usually associated with a family brand.

ETF families include the PowerShares and SPDR families previously mentioned. Additionally, there are dozens more ETF families you can easily find via an internet search. Investment companies offer ETFs in many styles within the family brand.

Mutual fund families include household names like Fidelity and Vanguard, as well as American Funds, Franklin Templeton, and T. Rowe Price, which make up the five largest mutual fund families at the time of this writing. However, there are literally hundreds of mutual fund families and thousands of mutual funds. The successful fund managers that you seek to hire are to be found throughout many different fund families.

Mutual fund families are variously organized. Some investment companies grew by acquiring smaller mutual fund companies and placing them under its family brand. In these families their different mutual funds may continue to operate independently with their own managers, research staffs, and investment philosophies. Other investment companies operate mutual funds that share a unified research staff with one investment philosophy, say, a "value" approach, and the family becomes known as a value house. Its funds may share portfolio managers who run, for example, both a large-cap fund and a small-cap fund, operating individually or on a team.

Some mutual fund investment companies have branched out to offer both a mutual fund family and an ETF family.

While no one mutual fund family has all the best managers, there can be certain advantages to investing in mutual funds from the same family:

- Break points, which are sales commission discounts based on your invested amount, can be based on the total amount invested in the fund family rather than in funds individually. Aggregating the amounts invested in the funds of the family allows you to reach higher breakpoint discounts, which reduces your sales commission.
- You can switch money from one mutual fund into another fund in the same family without incurring additional sales charges. This eliminates any sales charge when you rebalance your fund positions or rotate sectors.
- The sponsoring investment company may act, with the consent of the shareholders, to close a weak, underperforming fund and merge their investments into a larger fund in the same family. Such oversight would not be available with independent mutual funds.

Dollar cost averaging share boost

We introduced dollar cost averaging previously as a way to spread out your stock purchases and avoid an immediate drop in price that could follow a single purchase. Dollar cost averaging provides an additional benefit that is particularly relevant to the periodic purchase of mutual funds, such as in 401(k) and other retirement plans. When a mutual fund's price bounces up and down, with dollar cost averaging you end up purchasing more shares overtime than you might normally expect. The example in Table 5 shows how this works. Say, you payroll deduct $1,000 a month for your retirement plan, which is invested in just one mutual fund for the sake of demonstration. Over 21 months, the price of the mutual fund fluctuates from $10 down to $5, up to $15 and back down to $10. Recall that you can purchase fractional shares of a mutual fund.

In this example, we have invested a total of $21,000 at an average monthly purchase price of $10. We might have expected to have bought exactly 2,100 shares, however we have ended up with 2,303.125 shares.

Table 5   Dollar cost averaging share boost

Invested amount	Mutual fund share price	Mutual fund shares purchased
$1,000.00	$10.00	100.000
$1,000.00	$9.00	111.111
$1,000.00	$8.00	125.000
$1,000.00	$7.00	142.857
$1,000.00	$6.00	166.667
$1,000.00	$5.00	200.000
$1,000.00	$6.00	166.667
$1,000.00	$7.00	142.857
$1,000.00	$8.00	125.000
$1,000.00	$9.00	111.111
$1,000.00	$10.00	100.000
$1,000.00	$11.00	90.909
$1,000.00	$12.00	83.333
$1,000.00	$13.00	76.923
$1,000.00	$14.00	71.429
$1,000.00	$15.00	66.667
$1,000.00	$14.00	71.429
$1,000.00	$13.00	76.923
$1,000.00	$12.00	83.333
$1,000.00	$11.00	90.909
$1,000.00	$10.00	100.000

Total amount invested	Average of purchase prices	Total shares purchased
$21,000.00	$10.00	2,303.125

Effective price per share
$9.12

The extra shares happened because we bought many more shares as the price dropped down to $5. This more than makes up for the fewer shares we bought when the price ran up to $15. Compare the number of shares purchased at the $5 and $15 prices.

The dollar cost averaging share boost is a compelling reason to participate in your 401(k) and other retirement plans.

Note that this share boosting effect could also benefit you with stocks and ETFs, if you were to buy in periodic regular amounts in a long-term accumulation strategy.

Part Six

How to build your portfolio

R eview our discussion of selecting fund styles. Review also our discussion of risk, and review your goals.

We have already started building your portfolio with our outline for selecting fund styles. Building a portfolio follows the same steps as adding fund styles; only now we open the styles to include individual stocks and bonds. You will recall that we recommended starting with the U.S. domestic large-cap growth style. In that style, you can use a fund, or alternatively you can research and select individual stocks. For example, you could invest $20,000 in a U.S. large-cap growth ETF, or you can select ten domestic large-cap growth stocks and invest $2,000 in each. Or, you can use a combination of a fund and several stocks totaling $20,000. As you add the next style, U.S. small-cap stock growth, you can again use a mutual fund or several domestic small-cap stocks. Similarly for bond styles, you can mix a fund with individual bonds.

Your focus is to build a portfolio of securities that long-term will provide you a dependable income stream, whether for retirement, helping family members, traveling the world, or other goals. Recall the analogy of the buffet table we used to describe the various types of investment assets. Just as your main meal consists of the meat, vegetables, or casserole, your portfolio will consist primarily of stocks, bonds, mutual funds, and ETFs.

Diversification

In building your portfolio, use the outline we gave for adding styles. You will seek to reduce your overall risk by mixing and balancing complementary styles together for *diversification*. Diversification is essentially putting your eggs in many baskets and not all in one basket, or for our purpose in many styles. The various styles are each considered more are less risky, as we will discuss in detail.

For proper diversification we want our stocks, bonds, and funds to perform independently of each other as the economy moves through the business cycle. In other words, we want *uncorrelated* price movements. Recall the business cycle: early-recovery → expansion → full-employment → contraction → recession. Energy or information technology companies tend to do better during full employment and fare worse during recession, while consumer staples or medical care companies tend to hold up well during a recession and go quiet during full employment. The idea of diversification is that by owning companies in many different styles, at any stage of the business cycle some companies in your portfolio will do better even as other companies suffer. When the next stage of the business cycle comes, the companies and styles may reverse roles and different companies will support your portfolio. Diversification evens out the ups and downs of your overall portfolio, mitigating the severest drops in the value of your portfolio.

Diversification differs from sector rotation. Sector rotation tries to time the ups and downs of the business cycle and rotate through different sectors in concert with the business cycle. With a diversified portfolio we dispense with trying to time the business cycle, and we stay invested in many sectors all the time. We let the diversity of our companies protect us through the ups and downs of the business cycle.

We will now look at some complementary styles that you can balance against each other, because they tend to do well at different stages of the business cycle. While I will suggest allocation percentages for illustrative purposes, I recommend that you discuss your allocation strategy with your financial advisor.

Stock and bond styles

Your first and most important allocation is to determine the balance between stocks and bonds. Stock and bond prices in the past have often moved in different directions. For example, when the business cycle enters a recession, stock prices tend to fall. If the Federal Reserve then lowers interest rates to fight the recession, the lower interest rates would support or raise bond prices. At other times market unrest will be so great that it will pull down both stock and bond prices. Nonetheless, independent price performance provides a measure of safety for your portfolio.

Various studies have pointed to allocating 60% of your money to stocks and 40% to bonds as a middle ground. You can adjust toward a more aggressive portfolio by increasing the money to stocks and less to bonds, say in a 75%-25% allocation. Or, you can become more conservative with a 50%-50% allocation. As we discussed before, when you are young, you can be very aggressive and allocate 100% to stocks. In retirement, depending on your income needs and age, you may want to be more conservative by moving money into bonds, say 40% stocks and 60% bonds. You will always need a component of stocks to protect against inflation. As inflation pushes up a company's revenue and stock price, the company can raise its dividend payout to shareholders accordingly, maintaining a constant payout ratio.

In your early years of investing, you grow your wealth by accumulating the stock of growing companies. As you enter retirement and need to draw income from your investments, you look for stable companies paying dividends on their stock and interest on their bonds. Your allocation balance of stocks and bonds will shift over time: aggressive growth companies → growth companies → dividend-paying companies → corporate bonds →

government bonds. At any given time, your portfolio will be a mix of these styles. Over the years your emphasis will shift toward dividend-paying stocks and interest-paying bonds.

Large-cap, mid-cap, and small-cap stock styles

The size of a company affects how it performs through the different stages of the business cycle, so a natural divergence of stock styles is by size. Large companies have more financial resources, and they have more political influence with government bodies. Large companies also have internal bureaucracies, so they are slower to make decisions. Small companies can react more nimbly to opportunities, and they can lavish attention on fewer customers. Small companies often outperform during economic expansion.

A company's market capitalization is the product of its stock price times the number of outstanding shares of stock. Portfolio managers divide companies based on their market valuation into *large-cap*, *mid-cap*, or *small-cap* styles. Some portfolio managers combine small-cap and mid-cap together as smid-cap. The boundary between these capitalization styles varies widely among portfolio managers. Generally, most portfolio managers consider companies over $10 billion to be large-cap, and companies less than $1 billion to be small-cap. Companies with a capitalization between these extremes would be mid-cap. Various managers flex the boundaries between large-cap, mid-cap, or small-cap styles. For example, a small-cap manager may hold on to a successful company that has grown to become a large-cap company.

In your portfolio, you can balance large-cap style investments with small-cap or mid-cap style investments. Large-cap companies are generally considered less risky than small-cap companies, while small companies can grow faster than large companies. For the most part, your portfolio will be less risky if the large-cap style predominates the small-cap and mid-cap styles. As you start investing, I suggest you begin with the large-cap style and then add a bit in the small-cap or mid-cap styles aiming for a 90%-10%

split. As you gain confidence, you might be more aggressive and increase your portfolio risk and reward by going to a 70%-30% ratio of large-cap to small-cap and mid-cap.

Growth and value stock styles

A company and its stock is perceived as falling in the *growth* or *value* styles. Most stock funds become known for a growth or value style by virtue of the companies they invest in. A few funds try to strike a middle ground with a *core* or *blend* style.

Growth-oriented investors look for companies with innovative products driving revenue and profit growth. The company's economic engine is humming, and your evaluation shows a bright future. The fastest growing companies tend to be smaller companies who are expanding their sales to new customers. Aggressive investors may superemphasize rapid sales growth and temporarily forgo profits, for example at a start-up company. The growth investor is willing to buy sales growth with earnings to follow. He is willing to pay for stocks with a high P/E, stocks other investors might consider overpriced. Larger companies tend to grow moderately, because they often have already fully penetrated their markets and find fewer new customers to win over. For them the sales revenue from a new product is a small increment to their large revenue streams.

A rapidly growing company, on track to pay a future dividend, is a good candidate company for you. Large companies whose growth matches or beats the overall economy and who pay a healthy dividend are also good candidate companies. If a company's growth only matches overall economic growth and it doesn't pay a dividend, then you might do better elsewhere.

Value-oriented investors look for companies that they believe have stock prices undeservedly below the "true" value of the company. They expect the stock price to correct and go up. Value investors have to be patient while waiting for the correction, which may be a long time in coming. It helps if the value company pays a dividend, so the investor gets "paid to wait." The value investor looks for hidden value manifest in a low price, so he buys stocks when they are cheap with a low P/E. Investing in a dividend-paying value company is considered a conservative stock strategy.

Yet, while patience is a virtue, you must beware of companies known as *value traps*, whose stock prices never seem to reflect the unrecognized value. A troubled company, perceived as a value opportunity because its problems appear temporary, may not recover for years. Among funds, closed-end mutual funds which normally sell at a discount can be a value trap.

In the case of small-cap stocks, the growth style makes much more sense to me than the value style, because we buy small companies hoping they will grow into large companies. Small companies in the value style can be too much a short-term investment based mostly on price.

Growth and value styles are often paired in a portfolio to increase diversification, because growth stocks tend to perform well in a robust economy, while value stocks tend to perform better during a recession. So, if you invest in two U.S. large-cap stock funds, you would first invest in the growth style and then invest a little in the value style. For accumulating wealth, I favor the growth style over the value style by an allocation ratio of 67% to 33%.

Income style

Funds with the *income* style invest in a mix of dividend-paying stocks and interest-paying bonds. They hold large-cap stocks and investment-grade bonds. For diversification, income funds can be balanced against growth funds as you build up your assets. Income funds can be paired with bond funds in your retirement portfolio. The income style is generally considered a less risky, conservative style suitable for retirement portfolios. Also, the dividend-paying stocks will offer some protection against inflation through dividend increases, while bonds do not raise their coupon payments.

Short-term, intermediate-term, and long-term bond styles

In diversifying your portfolio, an allocation to bonds lends price stability to your portfolio, because the price of bonds tends to fluctuate much less than the price of stocks. Also, because bonds provide interest income, you may need to do less selling of securities for income, which makes you less vulnerable to market downturns.

Bond funds tend to specialize in *short-term*, *intermediate-term*, and *long-term* styles. Generally, short-term is considered to be under three years to maturity, intermediate-term from three to seven years, and long-term over seven years. A longer time to maturity normally correlates to a higher yield. Remember, a higher reward implies a higher risk. Long-term bond prices will swing more in response to prevailing interest rate changes than will short-term bond prices, so long-term bonds are riskier than short-term bonds.

You can start your bond holdings with the intermediate-term style. Depending on prevailing interest rates, you can allocate more or less to the short-term or long-term interest styles. Review our discussion of bond strategy.

Corporate, treasury, and municipal bond styles

Bond styles also derive from the issuers of bonds, with *corporate*, *treasury*, and *municipal* styles. U.S. treasuries are considered the safest investment and deemed "risk-free," despite one bond rating agency lowering the U.S. government to AA+ due to political gridlock in Washington, D.C. Municipal bonds are generally considered safer than comparably rated corporate bonds.

For some people, the greater consideration is the tax effect of these bond styles. Municipal bonds in taxable accounts have a tax-savings benefit that increases as you move up the income tax brackets. Review the discussion of taxation of municipal bonds. Consult with your tax advisor regarding the appropriateness of municipal bonds for you.

Your choice between the corporate or municipal styles depends almost entirely on your tax-adjusted return. Treasuries are for those who want maximum safety, at a lower return. Review our discussion of bond spreads.

Investment grade and high-yield bond styles

For the bond allocation in your portfolio, you should focus on funds and individual bonds in the *investment grade* style. Most bond funds invest primarily in investment grade bonds, but you should check the prospectus of each fund you consider. Some bond funds invest with a *high-yield* style, which means they invest in below investment grade junk bonds. If you have a large portfolio with substantial investment grade bond holdings, then you might consider adding a small allocation to a high-yield bond fund to boost your overall bond yield, say a ratio of 90% investment grade and 10% high-yield. But definitely avoid individual junk bonds.

Domestic and international styles

Once you have built your basic portfolio structure with the domestic styles described above, you can consider adding an international style overlaid on the stock and bond styles for added diversification, particularly if you have a very large portfolio. You can invest in companies based in the U.S., the *domestic* style, or in companies based outside of the U.S. through funds with the *international* style (outside the U.S.) or the *global* style (U.S. and international). International investments can be further divided between countries with developed markets like Germany, Japan, France, Great Britain, and Australia, which is the *foreign-developed* style; or countries with emerging economies like Poland, Egypt, Indonesia, and Argentina, which is the *emerging-market* style. Some large economies such as China and Brazil are still viewed as emerging market, despite their size.

Investing with the international style for bonds and stocks can be a lower priority for you. There are two main reasons. First, most large-cap companies are multinational corporations that do business around the world. As you invest in domestic large-cap companies, you will automatically gain international exposure for your portfolio. The other reason is that the big domestic large-cap mutual funds, in addition to investing in U.S. multinational companies, will often have the discretion to invest a small portion of their money directly in foreign multinational companies.

So, you are already likely to have international exposure even in your domestic portfolio.

For most people, the best approach to investing internationally is to use mutual funds or ETFs. Actively managed mutual funds will often have portfolio managers and analysts living in the foreign countries closely studying the companies and the local environment they operate in. Unless you are familiar with the laws and politics of a foreign county, their accounting rules, and the dynamics of their economy, you would be better served by professional portfolio managers.

On the other hand, many large foreign multinational companies like Toyota Motor Corp., Nestle SA, or Bayer AG are very familiar to you and me, we know and use their products. The stock of these and many other well-known foreign companies can be purchased on U.S. stock exchanges in the form of the *American depository receipt* (ADR). A U.S. bank purchases and holds a foreign company's stock and issues the ADR which is a package of the stock. One ADR represents some fixed number of shares of stock deposited at the bank, for example one ADR might comprise six shares of the underlying stock. The ADR trades on the exchanges like a regular stock and pays foreign dividends in U.S. dollars.

As you research foreign stocks, you will also have to evaluate specific country risk: The price of a foreign stock will be affected by the exchange rate between the foreign currency and the U.S. dollar. Political risk is unpredictable, as exemplified by the 2016 vote in Great Britain to exit the European Union, which introduced great uncertainty into markets. The economic stability of a foreign country itself may be questionable. For example, the periodic collapse of oil prices has thrown the economies of some oil-producing countries into crisis.

As you build your portfolio, you may want to limit the international style to no more than 15% of your stock holdings, since your domestic large-cap funds likely will include a portion of foreign stocks. A fund with the *international large-cap growth stock* style is a good place to start your international investing. For international bonds, I suggest that you only use mutual funds and ETFs and that you keep foreign bonds to no more than 10% of your bond holdings.

Sector and geographic styles

Building your portfolio with the styles described above will give you well diversified stocks, bonds, and funds. If you have a very wealthy portfolio, you could look to add a small allocation, say a cumulative 15%, to sector funds or geographic funds to try to boost your portfolio performance.

As an example, the international style can be further divided along geographic borders, with styles specific to a region like Europe or Asia, or to a specific country like Germany or South Korea. So, if you do your homework and believe that the economy of Canada or Poland will do particularly well, or you want to invest in the growth of China, you might buy such a fund. You will bear the increased risk of being concentrated in one foreign country.

Business *sectors* comprise companies who provide similar products and services, and, more often than not, compete against each other. Examples of sectors are industrials, technology, healthcare, energy, financials, real estate, consumer staples (such as household cleaning products, food, and diapers), and consumer discretionary (such as painting supplies, furniture, automobiles, and vacation travel). If you believe, as many people do, that technology is the future, you can choose from many such funds or companies. You can invest in the revitalization of U.S. manufacturing with an industrials sector fund. Just remember that the narrower the sector, the more concentrated is your risk.

Various other styles

In addition to the fundamental styles listed above, mutual fund and ETF sponsors have created many other themes for investing styles. A sampling of these styles is listed below.

- *Target date*: As the date (presumably retirement) approaches when the money will be needed, the fund switches from growth investments to less risky investments to focus on preservation of capital, that is from stocks to bonds. In general, this style is inflexible, not accounting for your personal risk preferences and your level of wealth.

- *Distressed stock*: Invests in troubled companies trying to turnaround. Very risky.

- *Commodity*: Precious metals, corn, oil, natural gas, soy beans, minerals, livestock, coffee, and commodity futures. Very risky.

- *Merger and acquisition* (M&A): Buys the stock of M&A candidates upon speculation or upon first announcement, anticipating a jump in the stock price when the deal is completed. One risk is waiting for a deal that eventually may fall apart.

- *Event driven*: Investing based on a recent or anticipated event that may act as a catalyst for a specific company's stock price.

- *Inflation protected*: Buys investments believed to hold up well with inflation.

You can generally avoid these and other unusual funds for your portfolio. They are either too risky or difficult to personalize to your situation. Also, review the discussion of exotic ETFs.

Adjusting your investment styles and risk over time

Review our discussion of your personal risk tolerance. Your allocation of money to the various styles can change as you grow older. Though people generally become more conservative nearing retirement, you need to steer your own course given your personal risk tolerance and level of wealth. If you are wealthy enough to ride out market downturns, then your portfolio could withstand more risk, even if your personal risk tolerance can not. Over your investment lifetime:

- Start saving and investing as early as you are ready. The sooner you get on (and stay on) the compound earnings track, the more wealth you will attain.
- While you are young, build up your risk tolerance. Don't be fearful and too conservative by putting all your money in CD's, money market funds, or bond funds that have little potential for capital appreciation. While young, you have more to lose from missing years of investment growth than from actual capital losses.
- Start investing with growth stocks and funds to build up your assets. Stay predominantly in stocks as you grow your assets.
- Use a buy-and-hold strategy, resist the temptation to trade too much.
- As you grow older, your allocation mix of stocks and bonds will shift over time: aggressive growth companies → growth companies → dividend-paying companies → corporate bonds → government bonds.

- In retirement, don't allocate any more to bonds than you need to generate sufficient income and maintain peace of mind. Use dividend-paying stock to keep up with inflation.
- If you have built great wealth, you can lean even more toward dividend-paying stocks and less toward bonds.

Adjusting portfolio risk

When you want to increase growth or reduce your risk, you have two ways to adjust the risk-reward potential in your portfolio.

- The primary method is to change the allocation ratio between the stock and bond styles. Shifting more toward growth company stocks while reducing bonds will increase the potential for stock appreciation with a corresponding increase in risk. Conversely, reducing investment in stocks while adding to bonds will decrease the potential for growth, while reducing the risk of capital loss.
- The second way is to adjust your styles within stocks or bonds. You can purchase more or less aggressive stocks, or less or more risky bonds, while leaving the allocation between stocks and bonds the same. For example, you can purchase small-cap growth stocks in place of large-cap. The small-cap companies tend to have greater growth potential, but they are riskier. Or you can replace corporate bonds with U.S. treasuries to reduce risk, but with lower yields.

These two methods can be implemented with individual stocks, bonds, or funds. In raising risk, I recommend allocating more to the large-cap stock style rather than switching to the riskier small-cap stock style. You could do a little of each method to leave your overall risk about the same. For example, you can add to your stock allocation reducing bonds, which increases risk, while simultaneously replacing some corporate bonds with U.S. treasuries, which reduces risk.

Start with small shifts in your mix and match of styles. Over time as you feel more comfortable, you can try moderately larger shifts. I suggest staying within the allocation ratios we discussed before. Also, you may want to consult with your financial advisor.

At this point, you now have the foundation you need to become a successful fundamental investor. If you follow the ideas and steps you have learned to this point, you can begin to invest to gain experience. You have the basic knowledge you need to start selecting individual stocks, bonds, and funds; and you have the guidelines you need to diversify your portfolio by allocating your money into the various investment styles.

Asset allocation through modern portfolio theory

We turn now to a method that financial services companies and institutions use to optimize the risk-reward trade-off for themselves and their clients. Asset allocation through modern portfolio theory is an attempt to optimize the risk-reward trade-off through sophisticated statistics. We will look at how it works and how you might use it with the help of your financial advisor.

Modern portfolio theory

Modern portfolio theory uses statistical analysis of historical performance data, through computer modeling, to optimize the allocation of money to the various investment styles. For any given target rate of return, the computer program seeks the specific portfolio with percentage splits of money among the styles that result in the lowest associated risk, defined as the portfolio with the least volatility in its returns and valuation. When a target rate of return is matched to its lowest risk portfolio, we say that the portfolio lies on the *efficient frontier*. Once you implement the optimal asset allocation of the efficient frontier portfolio, your actual return could be higher or lower than the target expected return.

Modern portfolio theory defines the risk of an investment to be the *volatility* of its returns, expressed as standard deviation. Volatility is a result of the market-driven swinging of prices up and down. Defining investing risk as volatility makes sense for a financial institution, like an insurance company, where they have constant flows of premiums into and payments out of their portfolio. Extreme swings in asset returns and prices can hurt them as they constantly buy and sell securities. Financial institutions have an infinite and constant time horizon; they do not have a single approaching date, like your retirement date, when the money will be needed. You will find that this definition of risk as volatility pervades the investment industry and media. When you listen to comments from investment professionals, bear in mind they view risk as volatility.

However, for you and me with a buy-and-hold strategy, a more appropriate definition of risk is the likelihood that we will have to sell a security at a loss. We care little about the ups and downs of a good company's return or stock price in the intervening years. For us, average earnings growth and dividend growth are more important. This misalignment of risk limits the benefit of the reduced volatility from asset allocation through modern portfolio theory for the individual investor; we will not be constantly buying and selling like a financial institution. Notwithstanding this limitation, asset allocation using modern portfolio theory is still an appropriate start to diversification. For individuals, the allocation must be adjusted for your personal risk tolerance and for the length of time until you need to use the money.

Modern portfolio theory is the source of much investing jargon, terms like *alpha*, *beta*, and volatility, which are popular in the profession and in the media. Alpha and beta describe aspects of portfolio performance relative to market performance as represented by some index. Beta compares the volatility of a fund to the volatility of the market index. A beta greater than one implies that a portfolio makes larger swings up and down than the market index does. A beta less than one implies the portfolio swings less than the market index does. Do not confuse beta with growth: A stock having a high beta does not necessarily mean it is a high growth stock. Alpha is a measure of risk-adjusted return, where a positive alpha implies a return better than expected for the amount of risk, and higher positive alpha is better. Negative alpha implies risk-adjusted return worse than expected. When you run across alpha and beta calculated for a fund or an individual stock, use them as one consideration in your own thorough analysis of that stock or fund.

Asset allocation as a service

Asset allocation through modern portfolio theory, or simply *asset allocation*, is a popular service offered by financial services companies. It has been packaged into programs for financial advisors to use with clients.

But first, we need to dispel some common marketing myths. You will at some point see marketing materials and media articles claiming that asset allocation accounts for 93% of the variance in a portfolio's performance, implying that asset allocation is the primary determinant of performance. This is a misinterpretation of a seminal study on asset allocation that has been seized upon by marketers of financial services and the media. The misinterpretation has been used to claim that stock selection by professional managers adds little value, and therefore you should use asset allocation with low cost index funds. A better statement of what the study found is that for professionally managed pension funds where the portfolio managers were similarly skilled, a fund's performance closely aligned with the asset allocation of the pension fund. Good stock and bond selection, whether by individual fund managers or by an index's selection committee, is a necessary complement to asset allocation to gain optimal performance.

You will also see modern portfolio theory misapplied when marketing presentations compare a portfolio of stocks and bonds to a portfolio of stocks, bonds, plus alternative investments. The claim is that adding alternative investments will reduce the volatility and make your portfolio safer. This presentation is misleading, because adding any third uncorrelated investment style will reduce volatility; the reduction is a statistical artifact. Adding a risky, speculative hedge fund to your stocks and bonds may reduce mathematical volatility, but you will face the increased likelihood of taking a loss on that risky hedge fund in place of safer stocks or bonds.

Having dispensed with such marketing claims, let's look at asset allocation as a professional service.

A financial advisor will try to learn as much as she can about you, your finances, your risk behavior, and your financial goals. When she produces an asset allocation report for you, the detailed recommendations will reflect the best thinking of the firm's economists and security analysts. Your financial advisor will personalize the recommendations, taking into account her understanding of your risk tolerance and the other information you have given her. The resulting portfolio will use the highest level of risk you are comfortable with to offer the corresponding highest expected return to meet your goals. You may find that to reach your goals you will need to invest more aggressively, taking on more risk than you want. Your financial advisor can help you make that decision.

Asset allocation has become a standard tool in the financial services industry. You can now find asset allocation calculators on various websites. If you run several calculators and answer their questions, you may get differing asset allocations recommended for you. The results differ because these calculators are highly sensitive to the underlying economic assumptions programmed into them based on the different outlooks of the economists at the financial institutions. You should simply view each result as representing one economist's opinion and use them as reference points for your own considerations.

Rebalancing your portfolio

Your asset allocation will need to be maintained. The financial services firm and your financial advisor should provide a *rebalancing* service to help you.

After you set up an efficient portfolio, its securities' prices will go up or down over time. Eventually, market action will cause your portfolio to drift off the efficient frontier, and your portfolio will no longer have the original expected target return and optimal asset allocation. If stocks do well and increase their share of the portfolio relative to bonds, the portfolio will take on proportionally more risk. If stocks do poorly, then their share will decrease and the portfolio will become more conservative with less risk, and the expected return will drop accordingly. Similarly, if the bond portion of the portfolio goes up or down, then the risk goes down or up respectively.

You should periodically rebalance your portfolio to push it back onto the efficient frontier. Rebalancing involves selling the portion of securities that have grown and exceed their efficient allocation and buying those securities that have fallen below their efficient allocation. For example, say, you originally allocated 20% of your total portfolio to small-cap stocks, and small-cap stocks have excelled and grown to 35%. You would rebalance by selling the 15% excess small-cap stocks, resetting the allocation to 20%. With the proceeds from the sale, you would buy bonds and any other styles that have fallen below their original allocation percentages, bringing them back up to their efficient allocations.

An important consideration is when to rebalance. Rebalancing services provide multiple ways to trigger an automatic rebalancing of your portfolio. One method triggers a rebalancing when a style allocation moves out of a preset range. In the previous example, the small-cap style allocation was set to 20% with a range from 5% to 35%. Whenever the allocation falls below 5% or exceeds 35%, a rebalancing is triggered. During a rebalancing, all the winning styles are sold and all the lagging styles are bought, resetting all styles to their original allocation percentages. A second triggering method is to rebalance your portfolio periodically, say, semiannually or annually. These methods can be combined, where once a year the software checks and performs a rebalancing only if any style allocation is out of its preset range. Finally, you could forgo automatic rebalancing altogether, and your financial advisor can manually trigger a rebalancing per some other strategy.

Various analyses of rebalancing have found no ideal triggering strategy. In choosing your rebalancing strategy, you will want to consider the pros and cons of rebalancing.

Pros:

- Rebalancing places you back in the efficient frontier portfolio for your chosen level of risk. You will have the highest target expected return for your assumed risk.
- Rebalancing enforces a discipline of selling high and buying low. You sell styles that they have gone up above their original allocations when their prices are higher, and you buy the styles that have fallen below their allocations when their prices are lower.

- Rebalancing sets you up for the turning of the business cycle, when the winning styles may fall back and the losing styles may turn around and go up.

Cons:

- Poorly timed rebalancing can prematurely cut off gains from winning styles. It doesn't "let winners run."
- With rebalancing, you are selling winning styles only to buy losing styles.
- Rebalancing can incur capital gain taxes. You loose the benefit from compounding earnings on the amount paid to taxes.
- With rebalancing, the many sales and purchases of securities may incur transaction costs.

Overall, I prefer the combined strategy of checking once a year and rebalancing only if any style breeches its preset range. I think the ranges should be fairly wide to let the winning styles run up.

Tax planning for investing

The U.S. tax system is set up to favor the creation of wealth. The tax code favors security investments held long-term, tax-advantaged retirement accounts, and tax-free municipal bonds. Upon death, the step-up in the basis of assets is the ultimate tax break. In your tax planning you can take advantage of these wealth building tax breaks.

Your tax planning begins when you first set up your investment accounts. Your tax plan will be put into action as you place your securities in the correct tax buckets. Tax considerations affect the structure of your accounts, your choice of type of investment security, and where you place your securities. You select individual stocks, bonds, and funds as we have previously discussed.

In this general discussion of tax planning, we will focus on federal taxes. We will introduce the concept of tax buckets as a tool for tax planning. Federal tax law is convoluted and riddled with odd exceptions. Federal tax law is subject to change by the U.S. Congress. Much of the tax planning we discuss may be relevant to your state tax, however many individual states have their own differing tax systems. Consult with your tax advisor for your specific situation.

Investment taxes

You pay primarily two kinds of tax on your security investments: a tax on capital gains and a tax on investment income. The income or capital gains could be from your own stock and bond investing or be distributed to you from a fund.

For the very wealth, any investments passed on to your heirs may also be subject to an estate tax. Estate tax planning is complex and beyond the scope of this book. You should consult a tax attorney regarding your estate tax planning needs.

Capital gains tax

Long-term capital gains, or simply *capital gains*, are profits and losses from investments bought and held for more than a year before selling. Capital gains are taxed at lower rates than your regular income tax rates. Recognizing the benefit of long-term investing for creating wealth, the federal government provides this tax incentive to encourage long-term investing. You will want to qualify for the capital gains tax whenever reasonable, for example by holding a stock for over a year before trading it away.

Qualified dividends are also taxed at capital gains tax rates. Dividends become qualified once you own a stock long enough to meet certain holding periods per IRS rules. (Refer to the IRS instructions for your tax return.) This tax policy favors growth with dividend-paying stocks over interest-paying bonds.

Investment income tax

Your *investment income* comprises interest, ordinary dividends, and short-term capital gains, which are profits and losses from investments held one year or less. Your investment income is taxed at regular income tax rates, along with your wages, rents, pensions, and social security.

Note that taxable bond interest is taxed at regular income tax rates.

Despite the name, short-term capital gains are treated as investment income for tax purposes. The generic term "income" can include long-term capital gains. Obviously, this nomenclature has the potential to cause some confusion in tax discussions.

Capital loss unequal treatment

The tax on capital gains and losses from trading securities, both long-term and short-term, is not applied evenly. All capital gains are included in income and taxed, while not all capital losses can be subtracted from income to reduce your tax. Capital losses and capital gains are deliberately treated unequally.

As we have said, tax policy encourages wealth creation through long-term investing by favoring capital gains with a lower tax rate. The government goes even further by discouraging risky investing behavior. As of this writing, in any one tax year net capital losses are capped at $3,000 for tax purposes. This includes both long-term and short-term capital losses. Gross capital losses are first subtracted from gross capital gains, and any remaining capital losses up to $3,000 are then subtracted from other income. Net capital losses greater than $3,000 can be carried over into the next tax year, again subject to another $3,000 yearly cap.

Tax brackets and rates

Both the regular income tax and the capital gains tax are tiered in *tax brackets*. The brackets are income ranges that are taxed at successively higher *tax rates*. (I suggest you refer to an IRS income *Tax Rate Schedule* to follow this discussion.) To understand how the income tax is applied, imagine that you can pour your income into each income tax bracket. When the lowest tax bracket's range is filled, you pour your income into the next bracket, and so on until you run out of income. The money in each bracket is taxed at that bracket's tax rate. The tax rate of the highest bracket where you ran out of income is your *marginal tax rate*; your next dollar of income will be taxed at this marginal tax rate. Similarly, capital gains fall into capital gains tax brackets that have increasing tax rates. Generally, capital gains tax rates will be lower than income tax rates.

Tax buckets

The investment and retirement accounts that you open with your broker or employer will have different tax consequences. You will find it useful to think of your various accounts as different *tax buckets* into which you place your securities. Each of your investment or retirement accounts is a tax-free bucket, a tax-deferred bucket, or a capital gains bucket. You can open accounts of each kind of tax bucket as needed. Our discussion will focus on how to use tax buckets to maximize your after-tax return on your investments. (Do not confuse tax buckets and tax brackets; they are different concepts.)

Work with your broker or employer to determine which kinds of accounts you are eligible to set up and contribute to. Consult with your tax advisor about your specific tax situation, your contribution and deduction limits, and qualifying for tax-free distributions.

Tax-free buckets—Roth IRA, Roth 401(k)

The *Roth IRA* and the designated *Roth 401(k)*, *403(b)* or *457(b)* retirement accounts are what we will refer to as the *tax-free buckets*.

You can fund Roth accounts only with contributions from your wage income or your spouse's wage income. The IRS has set various annual contribution limits and income limits. The IRS adjusts these limits for each new tax year. The contributions are not tax deductible, so your contributions are *after-tax*, which means you have paid the income tax on the wages.

Once funds are inside a Roth account, no tax is paid on any trades inside the account. No tax is paid on interest, dividends, or mutual fund and ETF distributions you receive in the account. You must hold these accounts for at least five years and meet age and other IRS rules to qualify for tax-free distributions. Once you qualify, all future distributions of principal and gains from the account will be tax-free in your retirement.

Tax-deferred buckets—traditional IRA, 401(k)

The *traditional IRA, SEP IRA*, the regular *401(k)*, *403(b)*, or *457(b)* accounts, and other retirement plans are the *tax-deferred buckets*.

The contributions to these accounts come from your wage income or your spouse's wage income, plus any employer contributions. Various IRS income limits apply, as well as contribution limits (which are coordinated with the contribution limits for the Roth counterparts). Your traditional IRA contributions are tax-deductible, while SEP IRA and 401(k) etc. contributions are excluded from taxable income. All these contributions are referred to as *before-tax*, because the income tax is deferred until the money is distributed from the account. Tax-deferred means you owe a future tax.

No tax is paid when security trades are made inside these accounts, and no tax is paid on interest, dividends, or mutual fund and ETF distributions received in the account. All future retirement distributions to you of principal and gains will be taxed at regular income tax rates; capital gains tax rates do not apply. At the age of 70½, you generally must begin taking an annual *required minimum distribution* (RMD) from your tax-deferred accounts, so that the government can begin collecting the deferred income tax you owe.

Note that in order to get the tax advantages of retirement accounts in tax-deferred buckets or tax-free buckets, you commit to locking up your money and will not have access to it until you reach a minimum retirement age, typically 59½. Any premature withdrawals are subject to severe IRS penalties.

Capital gains buckets—regular investment accounts

Regular investment accounts are the *capital gains buckets*. Securities in these accounts may be eligible for favorable capital gains tax treatment. Capital gains buckets include nonretirement investment accounts at brokerages, mutual fund companies, banks, and credit unions, as well as company stock purchase plans with employers.

The money you use to fund these accounts is from after-tax wages or other sources such as rent, inheritance, or insurance settlement. The money in capital gains buckets is not encumbered by deferred income tax.

When you sell a security in a regular investment account, you have a *taxable event*, meaning it triggers a tax you will pay with your annual income tax return. In capital gains buckets, gains and losses on securities held for more than a year are taxed at capital gains tax rates, while gains and losses on securities held for one year or less are taxed at regular income tax rates. You pay no tax on withdrawals from these accounts.

The payments to you of interest from bonds, dividends from stock, and capital gain and income distributions from mutual funds and ETFs are taxable events in the capital gains bucket. You will pay the tax on these payments with your annual income tax return.

Comparison of tax buckets

The tax consequences of using the different tax buckets are best illustrated by tracing a representative sequence of investments, trades, and tax events through each type of tax bucket.

Let's consider four examples with the same investing sequence placed in different tax buckets. Each scenario starts with $10,000 pretax to contribute towards retirement. Your income tax rate is 25%, and your capital gains tax rate is 15%. In the sequence you have eight time periods when your investments gain 12% per period. For the sake of simplicity, we assume all the gains are from share price appreciation with no interest or dividends paid. The trades in each period qualify for capital gains treatment. At the end of a period, you pay any tax due and calculate each sequence's total value. We repeat the process for eight periods. At the end of the scenario, you distribute all the money from your account, paying any tax due on the distribution.

The four scenarios are listed here, and the results are displayed in Table 6.

- *Tax-free bucket in the form of a Roth 401(k)*: You pay $2,500 income tax on the $10,000 gross wages. Then you contribute $7,500 into the Roth 401(k). You invest the money. At the end of each period, no tax is due. You add the 12% gain to the principal and repeat the cycle. At the end of eight periods, you sell the investments, distribute the money, and pay no tax on the distribution.
- *Tax-deferred bucket in the form of a SEP IRA*: Your SEP IRA defers the income tax, which allows your employer to contribute the entire $10,000 into the SEP IRA. You invest the money. At the end of each period, no tax is due. You add the 12% gain to the principal and repeat the cycle. At the end of eight periods, you sell the investments, distribute the money, and pay regular income tax on the entire distributed amount.
- *Capital gains bucket in the form of a regular account, with a buy-and-hold strategy*: You pay $2,500 income tax on the $10,000 gross wages. Then you put $7,500 in the account. You buy an allocation of securities and hold all of them throughout the eight periods, accumulating the 12% unrealized gains in each period as security price increases. With no securities sold in a period, you pay no tax. At the end of eight periods, you sell and pay capital gains tax on your gains. You withdraw the money, and there is no tax on withdrawing the original $7,500 principal and gains.
- *Capital gains bucket in the form of a regular account, with a trading strategy*: You pay $2,500 income tax on the $10,000 gross wages. Then you put $7,500 in the account. In each period you buy and sell securities yielding a 12% gain. At the end of each period, you pay capital gains tax. At the end of eight periods, you withdraw the money, and there is no tax on withdrawing the original $7,500 principal and gains.

The Table 6 shows the results of placing the investment sequence in each tax bucket.

Table 6 Tax bucket comparison

Assume income tax rate of 25% and capital gains tax rate of 15%. Begin with $10,000 pretax wages. Investments earn 12% per period, and in taxable accounts qualify for capital gains tax. You reinvest the earnings.

	Tax-free bucket Roth 401(k)	Tax-deferred bucket SEP IRA	Capital gains bucket Regular account buy-and-hold	Capital gains bucket Regular account active trading
Starting pretax wage	$10,000	$10,000	$10,000	$10,000
Income tax on wage	-$2,500	$0	-$2,500	-$2,500
Beginning investment	$7,500	$10,000	$7,500	$7,500
Period 1 gain	$900	$1,200	$900	$900
Period 1 tax event	$0	$0	$0	-$135
Period 1 after tax net	$8,400	$11,200	$8,400	$8,265
Period 2 gain	$1,008	$1,344	$1,008	$992
Period 2 tax event	$0	$0	$0	-$149
Period 2 after tax net	$9,408	$12,544	$9,408	$9,108
Period 3 gain	$1,129	$1,505	$1,129	$1,093
Period 3 tax event	$0	$0	$0	-$164
Period 3 after tax net	$10,537	$14,049	$10,537	$10,037
Period 4 gain	$1,264	$1,686	$1,264	$1,204
Period 4 tax event	$0	$0	$0	-$181
Period 4 after tax net	$11,801	$15,735	$11,801	$11,060
Period 5 gain	$1,416	$1,888	$1,416	$1,327
Period 5 tax event	$0	$0	$0	-$199
Period 5 after tax net	$13,217	$17,623	$13,217	$12,188
Period 6 gain	$1,586	$2,115	$1,586	$1,463
Period 6 tax event	$0	$0	$0	-$219
Period 6 after tax net	$14,803	$19,738	$14,803	$13,432
Period 7 gain	$1,776	$2,369	$1,776	$1,612
Period 7 tax event	$0	$0	$0	-$242
Period 7 after tax net	$16,579	$22,107	$16,579	$14,802
Period 8 gain	$1,989	$2,653	$1,989	$1,776
Period 8 tax event	$0	$0	-$1,660	-$266
Period 8 after tax net	$18,568	$24,760	$16,908	$16,312
Tax at distribution	$0	-$6,190	$0	$0
Total net proceeds	**$18,568**	**$18,570**	**$16,908**	**$16,312**
Total tax paid	-$2,500	-$6,190	-$4,160	-$4,055
Total gross proceeds	$21,068	$24,760	$21,068	$20,367

The results from our four simulations show us that the two tax-advantaged buckets yield higher total net proceeds than the capital gains bucket with either a buy-and-hold strategy or a trading strategy. The tax-free bucket and the tax-deferred bucket yield the same total net proceeds. (The slight difference is due to rounding calculations to the nearest dollar). The tax-free bucket and the tax-deferred bucket are effectively equivalent for tax efficiency.

In the capital gains bucket, the buy-and-hold strategy yields more than the trading strategy. If we had made short-term trades taxed at ordinary income tax rates, the total net proceeds from a short-term trading strategy would be even lower.

So why does a buy-and-hold strategy provide a better tax result than a trading strategy in the capital gains bucket? It has to do with the compounding of earnings. The simulations show us that your net proceeds depend on the frequency of taxable events, that being the number of times you must pay income tax. You can see in Table 6 that in the buy-and-hold sequence, after paying the initial income tax on the wage, there is one taxable event when the securities are sold at the end of period eight. In the trading sequence, after the initial income tax, there are eight taxable events for the trades in each period when you must pay tax. Each time you pay tax, you lose the future compounding of earnings on that money paid for tax. In effect, the potential benefit of compounding earnings is transferred along with the tax paid to the government. Review the discussion of the power of compounding earnings.

The importance of minimizing the number of taxable events is shown most clearly when comparing the tax-free bucket to the capital gains bucket with a buy-and-hold strategy. In both simulations, the sequences are identical until the end, when the buy-and-hold securities are sold and tax is paid on the capital gains.

The negative tax consequence of frequent trading is yet another reason to favor long-term investing in capital gains buckets. Since there are no taxable events inside a tax-free or tax-deferred bucket, the negative tax effect of frequent trading does not occur in the tax-advantaged buckets.

How to save on taxes

Minimize the number of taxable events

The simulations clearly show us that to increase your net proceeds you need to reduce the number of taxable events. You should make the maximum contribution each year to your tax-free or tax-deferred buckets, where you have no taxable events. In a capital gains bucket, you use a buy-and-hold strategy to reduce taxable events.

You can reduce taxable events by placing your dividend-paying stocks and interest-paying bonds in tax-free or tax-deferred buckets. Similarly, mutual funds and ETFs that make periodic distributions can be put in tax-free or tax-deferred buckets. In a capital gains bucket each dividend, interest payment, or fund distribution you receive is a taxable event for which you have to pay tax with your annual tax return.

Choose your tax rate

How do you choose between contributing to a Roth account tax-free bucket or to a traditional IRA or 401(k) account tax-deferred bucket? You do so by estimating what your total taxable income and marginal tax rate will likely be when you distribute the money. If you expect to be in a lower tax bracket in retirement, then take your tax deduction now and defer paying tax until retirement. If you expect to have a higher taxable income in retirement, then skip the deduction and pay your income tax now at a lower tax rate.

For most young people with a low starting income, you should contribute to tax-free buckets, forgo the tax deduction for contributions, and pay the income tax now at a low tax rate. Later in your prime earning years, you should contribute to tax-deferred buckets and take the tax deduction while your income is high.

If it comes down to a blind guess about your future income and tax rate, I suggest that you choose the tax-free bucket and pay your tax now on the positive assumption that you will be successful in your career and in your investing, resulting in a high income in retirement.

Tax bracket smoothing

For some people with fluctuating income, *tax bracket smoothing* may keep you in a lower tax bracket. If your annual income fluctuates up and down across a tax bracket boundary, you may find yourself bouncing in some years to a higher marginal tax rate from a lower marginal tax rate. With tax bracket smoothing, you attempt to flatten out your income fluctuations to stay in the lower tax bracket.

You may be able to keep yourself in the lower bracket by pushing out some capital gains into the next year. You can do this by delaying the sale of securities with unrealized gains in a capital gains bucket until after the end of the tax year. You could, alternatively, harvest capital losses to offset your capital gains and stay in a lower tax bracket. *Tax loss harvesting* is the practice of selling securities with unrealized losses specifically for the tax benefit.

Another means to tax bracket smooth is to adjust your distributions from tax-deferred buckets. You can only adjust the amount that is above the required minimum distribution. If you receive taxable retirement distributions, you might adjust the amount of your distribution income each year to stay under a tax bracket boundary.

Tax bracket smoothing is most effective when you can keep your marginal tax rate for the following year in the lower bracket as well. That would be the case when you push income into a low income year. Otherwise, you will have merely delayed paying at the higher tax bracket rate into the next tax year.

Tax conversion

The *tax conversion* is a powerful tax savings tool. A favorable tax conversion occurs when income subject to one kind of tax is converted to another kind of tax with a lower tax rate. By far, the easiest tax conversion you can make is to hold a security in a capital gains bucket for more than a year, when you will convert the tax on any gain from the income tax rate to the favorable capital gains rate.

A favorable conversion occurs when you contribute to a tax-free bucket. Once you meet the IRS qualification rules, all future capital gains from securities in the tax-free bucket will be free of income tax, when the capital gains otherwise would have been subject to at least capital gains tax rates in a capital gains bucket. Similarly, when you convert a traditional IRA to a Roth IRA, all future capital gains in the Roth IRA will be tax-free, instead of being taxed as regular income in a traditional IRA. This conversion to a tax-free bucket is especially effective in a year when you have little income due to a break in employment, resulting in a lower marginal tax rate for that year. With the conversion you will pay tax at the regular income tax rate on the entire amount distributed and converted from the traditional IRA. This tax payment must not be paid with the funds from the IRA, but rather with other money from nonretirement savings. Any money you take out of the IRA and use to pay tax instead of converting to the Roth IRA is a step backward on your retirement savings timetable. Review the discussion of the retirement investment timetable.

Tax mistakes

Your most serious tax mistake would be failing to contribute to your tax-free buckets or tax-deferred buckets. You need to contribute to your 401(k) as soon as one is available from your employer. Also, contribute each year to your IRA.

A common beginner tax mistake is to avoid selling a security because you want to avoid paying the tax. Once you decide a stock or bond should be sold, you should sell it immediately. For all the reasons that you decided to sell, the stock or bond is more likely to loose value than gain. The only exception would be a very brief delay to convert to capital gain tax rates or for tax bracket smoothing.

You must be careful not to make inadvertently an unfavorable tax conversion. For example, you should not put tax-free municipal bonds in a tax-deferred bucket converting their interest payments from tax-free to income tax rates. This is on top of receiving lower municipal bond interest yields to begin with. If you buy municipal bonds, do so only in a capital gains bucket.

Placing styles in tax buckets

You should plan where to place your security styles to maximize your net proceeds. The following is a suggested guide for you to start placing styles in the appropriate tax buckets. In each style we usually include individual stocks and bonds along with mutual funds and ETFs, unless we specify funds only. Your asset allocation will use all three tax buckets for maximum tax efficiency.

Tax-free buckets—Roth IRA, Roth 401(k)

We place here high quality, safe investments; investments paying dividends or interest, which elsewhere would entail numerous taxable events; and growth securities you have the greatest confidence in. We want to avoid losses that interrupt the steady compounding of earnings.

1. U.S. large-cap stock dividend-paying
2. U.S. large-cap stock growth
3. U.S. small-cap stock growth, funds only
4. U.S. intermediate-term corporate bond—investment grade
5. U.S. long-term corporate bond—investment grade

The tax-free buckets may have estate planning advantages when ultimately rolled over into a Roth IRA.

Tax-deferred buckets—traditional IRA, 401(k)

We want more growth and investments that would have taxable events elsewhere. We want to avoid losses that interrupt the steady compounding of earnings.

1. U.S. large-cap stock growth
2. U.S. small-cap stock growth, funds only
3. U.S. large-cap stock income or dividend-paying
4. U.S. intermediate-term corporate bond—investment grade
5. U.S. mid-cap stock growth
6. U.S. long-term corporate bond—investment grade

The RMD requirement means that we will eventually have to sell securities to raise cash for the annual distributions.

Capital gains buckets—regular investment accounts

We place aggressive growth here, where any overall loss can be offset against noninvestment income (up to $3,000 annually).

1. U.S. large-cap stock growth or value
2. U.S. small-cap stock growth
3. International large-cap stock growth or value
4. U.S. mid-cap stock growth
5. Municipal tax-free bond
6. Targeted sectors—healthcare, technology, industrials, consumer discretionary, financial, etc., funds only
7. REITs
8. High-yield bond, funds only
9. Alternative investments
10. Hobby account—trading stocks or options

You might wonder about doing your hobby trading in a tax-deferred bucket to avoid the frequent taxable events. However, you are probably better off doing your high-risk trading in a capital gains bucket, where you can deduct losses up to $3,000 against other income in a down year.

Part Seven

Retirement
Building toward retirement

Review our discussion of adjusting your investment styles and risk over time.

A main thrust of our investment planning has been accumulating assets toward retirement. Building your portfolio for retirement is a steady process of accumulating dividend-paying and interest-paying stocks, bonds, mutual funds, and ETFs.

For retirement planning I recommend using a life expectancy of 99 years of age. In a long retirement you will need to continue to grow your assets, or at least maintain them, because you want your investment income to last your entire life. So, you will always need some allocation to dividend-paying stocks for the growth as well as the income they add to your portfolio.

If you have followed the style allocation strategy we have discussed, you will be well prepared for the transition into retirement.

Generating income in retirement

Before you retire, you should use a spreadsheet or a calculator to estimate how much you will spend in retirement and the pretax income
you will need to support that spending. Various retirement calculators are
available on the internet. Because their results may differ, you should try
out at least two. This will tell you roughly how much retirement income
you need to replace your wages.

The first source of replacement income will be your monthly social
security check. (Go to the Social Security website for more information.) Some people may have additional income from pensions from past
employment, while others may have income from an annuity. Generally,
social security, pensions, and annuities provide lifetime retirement income
that you won't outlive. (We will discuss annuities in a later section.)

Next, you can tap your investment portfolio for further income. You
start by redirecting bond interest toward retirement spending, instead of
reinvesting the interest in new securities. After redirecting bond interest,
if you need additional income, you redirect your stock dividends toward
spending, instead of reinvestment. By the time you retire, you likely will
have a large part of your stock allocated to dividend-paying stocks. If not
and you need more dividend income, you can reallocate more of your stock
holdings toward dividend-paying stocks for the added income. Finally, you
redirect mutual fund and ETF distributions to retirement spending.

When you spend your interest and dividends, you give up the reinvestment and compounding of earnings, so you will depend of stock price
appreciation from your growth style companies for future asset growth.

When your bond yields are higher than your stock dividend yields, you
can to a limited extent increase your portfolio income by adjusting your
allocation to increase bonds versus stocks. However, you should maintain

a sufficient allocation to stocks for their dividend appreciation to offset increases in your living expenses due to inflation.

Once your portfolio provides sufficient income, you can settle on that mix of stocks for continued growth and bonds for income. You generally shouldn't shift toward bonds any more than your income needs require.

Selling assets in retirement

If you find that you still need more income than social security, pension, and your portfolio can provide, you may need to sell some securities or take money out of the maturing bonds in your bond ladder each year as needed for living expenses. When you choose to liquidate assets from your portfolio, you step onto a slippery slope. In each year that you sell assets, your portfolio will shrink progressively faster. Each year the constant sales will become a larger percentage of the shrinking portfolio, accelerating its decline. A commonly quoted rule of thumb has been that you could sell up to 4% of your portfolio per year. However, there is no single strategy for selling, instead it depends on the market conditions. I believe you should try to sell in years when the market has moved higher and set aside some cash savings to avoid selling when the market has moved down, recognizing that it is not possible to predict the market highs and lows notwithstanding.

Ultimately, you may find your portfolio is too small to retire on. Rather than draw down your investment assets too much, I recommend you consider several other prudent steps: You could delay retirement for a few years. Each year you continue to work and save makes a big difference in the longevity of your portfolio. You could reduce what you spend in retirement to a sustainable level. You could take a part-time job in retirement to supplement your income. A part-time job can also have other benefits like being an activity you enjoy or providing social contact.

By starting to save and invest early in life, with proper investment planning as we have discussed, you won't have to face running out of money in retirement.

Annuity

An *annuity* is a contract between you and an insurance company to set up your own private pension plan. When you purchase an annuity, you buy a contract which is a promise by the insurance company to pay you in retirement an income stream for the rest of your life. Your annuity income will be taxed like pension income at regular income tax rates.

In purchasing an annuity, you own a contract. You do not own the investments listed in an annuity, such as any mutual funds or index funds. Instead, subaccounts of the annuity track the performance of the referenced mutual fund or index fund. The performance of your annuity may vary from that of the referenced funds due to the different expenses and fees applied. The income that you eventually receive comes actually from the insurance company's pool of investments.

An annuity, like other insurance products, shifts the burden of risk from you to the insurance company. For the premium you pay, the insurance company will assume the market risk of investing and pay you a retirement income for life, removing the risk to you of outliving that income. The insurance company combines your premium with that of other annuity buyers into a large investment pool, and over the years your annuity should grow in value. When you choose to start collecting your income, the current value of your annuity is annuitized, or converted, into an income stream for the rest of your life.

Annuities have many options, known as *riders*, that offer an array of extra features for additional premium cost. As an insurance-based product, an annuity can offer riders for a death benefit or for a guaranteed minimum income stream. You should buy riders very carefully, as the riders add substantially to the cost of the annuity.

During the annuity sales presentation, a salesman will show you a detailed *illustration*. It is called an illustration because it is not a guarantee or promise of future income; it merely shows you how annuity cash flows might pay out. The sales representative should explain all the various costs to you within the annuity contract.

Annuities are extremely complicated and expensive products. I recommend that you discuss any annuity proposal only with an advisor well-known to you, and who has your best interests at heart.

When you might consider an annuity

Annuities are not for everyone. I believe they are suitable for you only if you have specific needs that justify the high cost.

- *You want income that you won't outlive*: However, note that annuity income is not adjusted for inflation, so the annuity income's purchasing power will decline over the years.
- *You are extremely risk adverse*: You can not tolerate the swings up and down of a portfolio; it keeps you up at night. Then the guarantees you pay for in an annuity may give you some comfort.
- *You need discipline imposed on you*: If you know that you are likely to tap your retirement accounts prematurely for spending on expenses like vacations or cars or helping the kids, then you might lock up your money in an annuity. Once you annuitize your contract and start receiving your income, you can not change your mind and get more money out sooner.

When you would not want an annuity

You would look away from an annuity to a more suitable solution, when you want to avoid the following.

- *High fees*: Annuities have high costs including: premium cost, rider fees, mortality and expense (M&E) fees, administrative fees, investment management fees, and surrender charges. The ongoing cost of an annuity, depending on the added riders, may be two or three or more times the cost of a managed mutual fund.

- *No liquidity*: Your money in an annuity is intended to be locked up for future retirement income. You can not access it without a severe tax penalty on top of costly surrender charges to the insurance company. You will also have wasted the sales commission and M&E fees that you paid to set up and maintain your private pension plan.

- *Overly complicated investment*: Annuities are among the most complex investments with many moving parts. Moreover, after decades you might tend to forget the complicated details of an annuity and its riders, losing track of the benefits that you have purchased.

- *No inheritance for the kids*: Generally, an annuity income stream ends when you die (and your spouse, if a joint annuity), leaving nothing for your heirs. The annuity is not designed to be a vehicle for leaving an inheritance to your kids. Though a supplementary death benefit rider, purchased at an additional premium cost, could leave something for the kids, you have much better ways to prepare an inheritance for the kids. Consult with your financial advisor and estate attorney.

For most people, the investment process that we have discussed throughout this book would be a less expensive and less complicated way to prepare for retirement.

Hiring a financial advisor

As your wealth grows, you may find that you want expert help in specialized areas. We have mentioned several types of advisors: the financial advisor to help you select investments and develop an overall strategy; the tax accountant for tax guidance, tax returns, and to deal with the IRS; and the estate planning lawyer to structure trusts and wills. Each is an expert in his or her area, and together they work as your advisory team. We will focus here on finding a financial advisor.

A financial advisor can help you with any aspect of the investment process that we have discussed: your self-assessment; setting attainable goals; choosing stocks, bonds, and funds; asset allocation to styles; and the transition into retirement. He will have access to company research reports and investment recommendations from his analysts. Your financial advisor will have computerized tools to help you with your financial goals, asset allocation, and long-term planning for retirement.

Trust

Your most important decision in hiring a financial advisor is do you trust him with your money and your financial future. You want to find a financial advisor with your best interests at heart, which is not easy to ascertain in a short interview. All successful financial advisors have the sales skill to win a client's trust, whether by a record of investment results or by a confident personality. They must earn and maintain your trust over your entire relationship.

Many clients lean on a trusted financial advisor to reinforce their risk tolerance and help them through market recessions. An underappreciated benefit of working with a financial advisor is that he can help you avoid mistakes and save you from losing money. Your financial advisor can help you ride out market downturns, instead of selling in a panic. Few investors really know how they will react in extreme market downturns, when their own true risk tolerance is put to the test.

Before you interview financial advisors, you must look at yourself and determine if you will listen to and judiciously take advice from a financial advisor. If you have a habit of rejecting advice, then don't waste your time and theirs. Many financial advisors will "fire" clients that they can not help.

Fiduciary or broker

A financial advisor's duty toward her client is either as a *fiduciary* or as a *broker/agent*, and the duty owed will vary with the situation and financial advisor's role. *Financial advisor* is a broad title applied to many professionals in the investment industry including bankers, insurance agents, stock brokers, and investment advisors. Accountants or real estate agents might also use the title. In these roles the financial advisor can act as a broker/agent in a sales capacity or as a fiduciary in an investment advisory capacity. The same financial advisor, with the same client, may act in one instance as a broker/agent and in another instance as a fiduciary.

You should ask your financial advisor in what role she is acting, broker/agent or fiduciary, when you discuss a specific investment or strategy. You should also ask how she is compensated for selling any given investment.

Whenever a financial advisor acts as a broker/agent, she is selling you a product for which she receives a sales commission. This includes stocks, bonds, mutual funds, ETFs, as well as hedge funds, annuities, and life insurance. The cost to you of the sales commission will vary greatly with the specific product. A financial advisor acting as a broker/agent must recommend a product that is *suitable* for you. The suitability standard means the product meets your need and is not otherwise wrong for you. For example, she should sell investments to you only if they are suitable given what she knows about your portfolio (broadly diversified) and risk tolerance (low). So, if you want to buy a blue chip dividend-paying stock, she may determine that the stock is suitable for you and recommend you place an even larger order. If you want to buy a junk bond that is unsuitable, she should recommend against it, but, ultimately, as an agent she must follow your instructions.

A potential *conflict of interest* arises between the financial advisor and a client, when the financial advisor gets paid for selling an investment product and the commission grows with the size of the order. A salesman is motivated to sell you the product and more of it. She may also be tempted to suggest a different investment that, while still suitable for you, has a higher sales commission rate.

To remove this conflict of interest, the fiduciary standard requires the financial advisor to act in the best interests of the client, placing the client's interests ahead of the financial advisor's own interests. When acting as a fiduciary, the financial advisor's compensation will be fee-based, usually based on a percentage rate of the portfolio size or, perhaps, a flat hourly fee. The financial advisor sets her management fee as she feels justified by her expertise and level of service to you. This management fee, instead of a sales commission, eliminates the temptation to place frequent, sizable orders at high commission rates, because the financial advisor's compensation will not be affected.

Your financial advisor acts as fiduciary, when you grant her discretion to make trades for you in a managed account. Fund managers and investment managers also act as fiduciaries for their investors.

Fees

As you invest, you will pay for professional investment help through sales commissions or managed account fees or a mix of the two.

Review the previous discussions of bond pricing, mutual fund fees, and alternative investment fees.

Sales commissions and embedded sales charges

Typically, you will buy investments in accounts where the financial advisor is paid with sales commissions for his advice and service. This includes stocks and options, bonds, mutual funds and ETFs, hedge funds, and annuities. Different products have vastly different commission rates. The amount of the sales commission will depend on the commission rate of the product, the size of your order, and the financial institution where you place the order.

The sales commission can be in plain sight like an itemized sales charge for purchasing or selling a stock. Or, the sales commission can be built into the price, like bonds where the expenses and profit margin of the broker are included in the price quote when you buy or sell.

Whenever you buy an investment product or service, you should ask the financial advisor, stock or bond broker, or any sales representative how they will be paid. You have a right to know, and they are required to tell you. The sales commission is an important, variable cost in your choice of an investment and of the financial institution where you place the order.

Fee-based managed account

In a managed account you sign an agreement with a financial advisor who will watch over and manage your security investments. For those specific assets included under the management agreement, the financial advisor is compensated on a fee basis. The periodic fee will depend on the dollar size of the assets under management and on the financial advisor's fee schedule. The various managed accounts of a family may be aggregated in determining possibly a lower overall percentage fee.

Certain assets, for example buy-and-hold bonds, may be excluded from the management agreement and continue to be transacted with a sales commission. In that case, you will not pay an annual management fee on long-term bond holdings and instead pay a commission upon the infrequent bond trade.

As your investment manager the financial advisor acts as a fiduciary investing in your best interests. In a separately managed account you can give your financial advisor *discretion*, where you pre-authorize him to make decisions on your behalf. While you will take a less active role, you should still stay engaged. In a nondiscretionary managed account, your financial advisor needs to get your okay to a recommendation before making a trade.

The trend in the financial services industry is toward fee-based managed accounts. However, financial services companies have a minimum account size for managed accounts, usually $500,000 or possibly $250,000. Smaller accounts are served on a sales commission basis.

Managed account fees can be negotiated, particularly if you have a very large account that financial advisors will compete for. It never hurts to ask for a lower fee. Fees can range below 1% for very large accounts.

Components of total cost

When your financial advisor quotes a fee for a fee-based account, that fee is a part of the total cost to you of investing. The fee may cover one or more components of the total cost depending on the types of investments in the managed account. You should understand what components of total cost the fee covers and what costs may be in addition to the managed account fee. The three major components of cost generally break down as follows:

- Financial advisor cost: The financial advisor helps you formulate an asset allocation strategy, supervises your account, selects individual investments, hires investment managers and fund managers, monitors performance, and makes changes to investments or managers as needed. His cost is part of the managed account fee.

- Investment manager fee: When you and your financial advisor hire an investment manager in a separately managed account, he specializes in choosing stocks and bonds for your account. In a separately managed account, the stocks and bonds are held in your account and you own them directly. The manager charges a fee which is included, along with the financial advisor's fee, in the quoted managed account fee. Alternatively, a mutual fund or ETF held in a managed account will subtract its expenses directly from the return of the fund, so that the fund's operating costs are not included in the managed account fee, but are nonetheless a part of the total cost to you.

- Transactions costs: These comprise two sets of trading costs. One is the cost of trading mutual fund, ETFs, stocks, and bonds in your managed account; these sales costs are usually included in the managed account fee, so you would not be charged a sales commission. The other is the cost of trading securities at a fund; this cost is subtracted from the fund's return and not included in the fee for your managed account.

As you can see, the total cost of investing will be higher than the quoted managed account fee, when fund managers subtract their costs from the fund's return, and their costs are not included in the managed account fee. When you evaluate managed account programs, you should ask the financial advisor what is the total cost of investing to you when all costs are accounted for. He should be able to estimate the total cost to you based on the fee information from the mutual fund or the ETF. You can then compare true total costs.

You might also ask whether nominal fees, like IRA fees, online access fees, check writing fees, or other account maintenance fees, can be waived or included within the managed account fee.

Hidden cost of 401(k) plans

In some situations, cost can be very difficult to determine. This is often the case with the hidden cost to you of 401(k) and other retirement plans through your employer. When a company arranges with a financial institution to provide a 401(k) plan for its employees, the company can pay the full cost of administering the 401(k) or split the cost with the 401(k) participants. The mutual funds in retirement plans offer special share classes with varying expense fees for this purpose. The employer can select from share classes, such as Class R1, R2, or R3, where each class charges a different level of fees against the fund's return. These fees pay for part of the cost of running the 401(k) plan, with the company paying the balance. A generous employer may pay for all of the plan's cost, leaving a higher return for the employees. When a company can not afford the 401(k) plan's entire cost, then in order to provide a plan for its employees, it may choose to share the cost with participants through the expense fees of a Class R share.

When you change jobs to a new company, you should consider rolling your 401(k) into an IRA, where you will have better visibility of the costs. You will have direct control over your IRA, unlike a 401(k) which is controlled by your employer. An IRA at a large brokerage will also have more mutual funds and other investments for you to chose from.

Conclusion and new beginning

Investing success comes from learning and discipline. In these pages, I have given you the basic knowledge and insights to invest for a comfortable retirement and more. The fundamental analysis and long-term investing that we have discussed, given enough time, will work for you. Do your homework and build your portfolio with well-researched stocks, bonds, and funds. Reinvest dividends, interest, and earnings distributions. Let the compounding of earnings work for you by investing early while young, and don't set yourself back years on your investment timetable by prematurely withdrawing and spending your investment capital.

Discipline must come from you. We have discussed how different personality traits can help or hurt you as an investor.

You must resist the temptation to take shortcuts with newsletters or hapdictive charts touting stock tips. Disregard the hype of pundits and the bragging of friends. And after some successes of your own, avoid overconfidence in your forecasting abilities.

Hire professional help when you feel you need it. Hire investment advisors who practice the same fundamental analysis that we have discussed. Be willing to pay a reasonable fee to hire talent and for results.

Ultimately, investing will be a lifelong pursuit, learn to enjoy it and not be fearful. Take quiet pleasure in accumulating the income-producing investments that will secure your future.

Made in the USA
Columbia, SC
30 March 2018